DAUGHTER OF THE LEFT HAND

A Play

NORMAN HOLLAND

SAMUEL FRENCH

LONDON
NEW YORK SYDNEY TORONTO HOLLYWOOD

Copyright © 1972 by Norman Holland
All Rights Reserved

DAUGHTER OF THE LEFT HAND is fully protected under the copyright laws of the British Commonwealth, including Canada, the United States of America, and all other countries of the Copyright Union. All rights, including professional and amateur stage productions, recitation, lecturing, public reading, motion picture, radio broadcasting, television and the rights of translation into foreign languages are strictly reserved.

ISBN 978-0-573-01537-3

www.concordtheatricals.co.uk
www.concordtheatricals.com

For Amateur Production Enquiries

United Kingdom and World
excluding north america
licensing@concordtheatricals.co.uk
020-7054-7200

Each title is subject to availability from Concord Theatricals, depending upon country of performance.

CAUTION: Professional and amateur producers are hereby warned that *DAUGHTER OF THE LEFT HAND* is subject to a licensing fee. Publication of this play does not imply availability for performance. Both amateurs and professionals considering a production are strongly advised to apply to the appropriate agent before starting rehearsals, advertising, or booking a theatre. A licensing fee must be paid whether the title is presented for charity or gain and whether or not admission is charged.

The Professional Rights in this play are controlled by Samuel French Ltd (Concord Theatricals) Aldwych House, 71–91 Aldwych, London WC2B 4HN.

This work is published by Samuel French, an imprint of Concord Theatricals.

No one shall make any changes in this title for the purpose of production. No part of this book may be reproduced, stored in a retrieval system, or transmitted in any form, by any means, now known or yet to be invented, including mechanical, electronic, photocopying, recording, videotaping, or otherwise, without the prior written permission of the publisher. No one shall upload this title, or part of this title, to any social media websites.

The right of Norman Holland to be identified as author of this work has been asserted in accordance with Section 77 of the Copyright, Designs and Patents Act 1988.

DAUGHTER OF THE LEFT HAND was first produced by the WARRINGTON CO-OPERATIVE DRAMA GROUP on 2nd May 1972, with the following cast:

Maggie Walters an upper servant	*Sylvia Rothwell*
Rev. Randall Cooper	*Michael Hall*
Harriet Hallam	*Jean Alcock*
Lesley Hallam	*Heather Puddephatt*
Mildred Drew	*Sheila Horswill*
Vivian Hallam	*Kenneth Ward*
Rex Hallam	*Allan Taylor*
Lillah a parlourmaid	*Connie le Personne*
Nicola	*Kathryn James*
Vashti Kemp-Collet	*Phyllis Henderson*

The play produced by **Trevor Robinson**

Set designed by **Len Rowland**

Costumes by **Trevor Robinson**

For his performance as Rex Hallam, Allan Taylor received the "Actor of the Year" Award presented by the *Manchester Evening News*.

The action of the play passes in the drawing-room of Rex Hallam's house, Stanton Manor, Medham, about twenty miles from London.

ACT I Scene 1	A Wednesday afternoon in May
ACT I Scene 2	Friday evening
ACT II Scene 1	Saturday morning
ACT II Scene 2	Sunday morning

Time—1903

For
Stanley Richards
With Affection
and
With Admiration

DAUGHTER OF THE LEFT HAND

ACT I

SCENE 1

The drawing-room of Rex Hallam's house, Stanton Moor, Medham, about twenty miles from London. A Wednesday afternoon in May, 1903.

It is a pleasant, airy room which is looking its best in the light of this May afternoon. In the rear wall is a double door set at an angle across the corner of the room. To one side of it is a console table bearing a flower arrangement and to the other a china cabinet. There is a lace-curtained bay window with a window-seat and heavy floor-length curtains. In one wall there is another, less imposing, door. Above the china cabinet is the portrait of a sweet-faced woman of thirty or thereabouts wearing a dress of the late Victorian era. Around the walls are two or three pleasing but undistinguished water-colours. There is a secretaire, with a bell-push in the wall above it.

Daylight throughout has that blazing, golden quality of the Edwardian heyday. By night the gas chandelier, centrally suspended, sheds its peculiar greeny-yellow glow which imparts its own curious significance to the setting

Maggie Walters, an upper servant in late middle-age, ushers in Randall Cooper, a clergyman of forty odd, who is carrying an envelope rather larger than correspondence size

Maggie If you'll just wait a minute, Mr Cooper, I'll tell Miss Harriet you're here.
Randall You needn't disturb her, Maggie. I just wanted to leave this (*indicating the envelope*) for Colonel Hallam.
Maggie I'm quite sure that Miss Harriet would much prefer to be disturbed, sir. (*Reproachfully*) It wouldn't be right if her fiancé called and left without a word, would it?
Randall No. No, I suppose it wouldn't. (*He reflects briefly*) Yes, you'd better tell her I'm here, Maggie. (*Moodily, he walks to the window and stands looking out*)

Maggie regards him with a puzzled expression

Harriet Hallam enters by the double door. She is thirty years of age, has something of a spinsterish air, and the habitual severity of her features is emphasized by a simply-cut black dress. A chatelaine, hanging from her belt, proclaims her authority as family housekeeper. Randall turns at her entry and her expression is almost radiant as she hurries towards him with hands outstretched in greeting

Harriet Randall! Lesley told me you'd arrived. I simply rushed down . . .

Randall is forced to take her hands in his—somewhat hampered by the envelope

Maggie smiles at them as she goes out by the double door

How are you, Randall?
Randall I'm very well, Harriet. How are you?
Harriet All the better for seeing you.

She glances over her shoulder to make sure that Maggie has gone and then swoops forward and kisses him. Then, with a little cry of mingled frustration and longing, she embraces him and places her cheek against his. Less spontaneously, Randall puts his arms about her

Why is it always like this?
Randall Like what?
Harriet With me doing all the wooing and you scarcely noticing that I'm here.
Randall Don't say that, Harriet. You must make allowances. I've told you it will take time for me to get accustomed to the idea . . .
Harriet Oh, I've made allowances until I'm tired! (*She frees herself, walks away and then wheels suddenly on him*) What was she like?
Randall She?
Harriet You know—Kathleen, your dear, dead, devoted wife.
Randall Oh, don't please, Harriet . . .
Harriet (*remorselessly*) What was she like?
Randall You've seen her picture.
Harriet It tells me nothing. There's only a moony face, big eyes and a pouting rosebud of a mouth. She could have been anybody—or nobody.
Randall (*kindling*) She was somebody. Oh, Kathleen was certainly somebody—a person and an individual. She was loving and lovable and she had a considerable talent for helplessness which she somehow made amusing. She was a gay, touching, endearing creature.
Harriet Not a bit like me.
Randall (*too quickly*) Not in the least. (*Recovering*) I mean you're quite, quite different. You're so—so self-reliant. Kathleen was often afraid of life.

(*She sits in the armchair and looks troubled and reflective.*)

Harriet Oh, I'm afraid all right. I'm terrified sometimes. Especially when I consider that so much of my life is over with nothing to show for it. But I was never afraid with Gregory. (*She pauses watching him closely* *for a reaction which does not materialize*) Don't you want to hear about him?

Randall Not unless you want to tell me.

Harriet Don't you at least want to know where I met him?

Randall (*incuriously*) Where did you meet?

Harriet It was when I went to stay with Aunt Jessie in Bristol six years ago this summer. I met him the second day of my visit and almost every day thereafter. We could not bear to be apart. For seven months we were ideally happy.

Randall Why didn't you get married?

Harriet He had a wife already.

Randall I see.

Harriet They were unsuited. They lived apart. (*She rises.*) Are you shocked, Randall? (*Moving hopefully towards him*) Perhaps a little jealous?

Randall (*withdrawing*) No, no. You were younger then. You didn't appreciate the seriousness of what you were doing.

Harriet Oh yes, I did. And I'd do the same again in similar circumstances. (*She folds her arms as if embracing herself*) Oh, it warms my heart to speak of Gregory. He was demanding and demonstrative—ardent and demonstrative. Everything, I'm afraid, that you are not. (*She sighs*) So you see, we're each other's second best and we've got to make the best of one another.

Randall You're quite right, Harriet. Once I've seen Stephen safely through Cambridge . . . (*He goes over to the window as if seeking a refuge*)

Harriet But that will take years! I want to have my children before I'm too old.

Randall (*shaken*) Children? You want children?

Harriet Isn't that one of the purposes of marriage mentioned in the sacrament? Don't you want children—our children?

Randall Yes. Yes, of course. (*But it is clear that the idea disturbs him and he is further troubled by her probing regard. Desperately, he shifts his ground*) I am sorry you find me undemonstrative. I expect you find me dull, too.

Harriet No, Randall. You're not really dull.

Randall Coming here means a great deal to me.

Harriet It's something to know that.

Randall You're such a united family. There's such warmth here and so much kindliness. And then there's your father . . .

Harriet (*with a hint of sarcasm*) Oh yes, don't forget Father. He's by far the most interesting of us.

Randall He's such a help to me as Vicar's Warden. I don't know what I should do without him. Why, he even helps me with my sermons.

Harriet I know. I know. Sometimes he reads them to me. It hardly seems fair that I should have to hear them twice.

Randall I brought next Sunday's sermon. (*He gives her the envelope*) Would you ask your father if he would glance through it?

Harriet Of course. (*She goes to the secretaire and places the envelope on it*)

You know, Father's delivery of your sermons is a great improvement on yours.
Randall Indeed?
Harriet He gets so much more feeling into the words.
Randall I'm sure he does. He's the most remarkable man I've ever met—and the truest Christian. The words most often on his lips—
Harriet —are, "The truth can't hurt us."
Randall It's a wonderful creed to live by, Harriet.
Harriet I'm sure it is—and Father *does* live by it.
Randall (*enthusiastically*) Oh, he does! He does! Do you know what I discovered yesterday? In spite of everything, he's doing all he can to help Fletcher to a new situation.
Harriet That's like Father. (*Coming down to him again*) And why shouldn't he help Fletcher?
Randall I should think that's obvious. A butler who behaves as Fletcher did is not to be trusted.
Harriet Because he had an affair with one of the maids? Butlers often do. It's one of their prerogatives.
Randall Harriet!
Harriet Well, it is! (*She moves away and sits on the couch*) I don't suppose Father would have minded if he hadn't actually caught them at two o'clock in the morning.
Randall I don't like to hear you speak in this vein, Harriet. You are being flippant about a serious matter.
Harriet No, I'm not. I'm pointing out that butlers and maids are human beings of opposite sexes and sometimes they can't help acknowledging the fact. I'll never forget the night Father discovered them. Never as long as I live.
Randall You shouldn't dwell on such things. It isn't right that you should.
Harriet Why not? We get so little excitement and this was tremendously exciting. (*She turns away from him, her face becoming increasingly animated as she recalls the episode*) We heard Lillah's scream and then men shouting. We rushed downstairs and there was Lillah, in her nightdress if you please, crying her eyes out. Fletcher was standing, pale-faced and shaking, with Father in between them looking as stern as a judge.
Randall How disgusting! It must have been an utterly degrading spectacle.
Harriet It wasn't, I assure you. But it was all over so quickly. Father was magnificent. He ordered everybody back to bed immediately. It was—thrilling! I saw what Father must have been in the War. He wasn't the City magnate then. He was Colonel Hallam of Gascoigne's Horse and everybody obeyed him instantly. Instantly!
Randall I don't know why you store up details of this sordid business.
Harriet I've told you. It was an event. In this house now we measure time from the moment of Fletcher's departure. We didn't see him again. He left first thing in the morning. Somehow, I feel that he had been harshly treated. Lillah should have been dismissed as well. She, surely, was at least as much to blame.
Randall I don't agree. Your father acted wisely. She's a young girl. Fletcher

was not only her senior in years and situation but he was, supposedly, a religious man though, of course, a Nonconformist. He abused his position and led the girl astray.
Harriet I'm sure he didn't. Have you ever noticed the way Lillah looks at men? At Vivian in particular? I think Father ought to get rid of her.
Randall That is for your father to decide. Women are notoriously harsh in judging their own sex. You will oblige me by not mentioning this unfortunate incident again. It is something which manifestly should not be discussed between two persons of opposite sexes—even if they do happen to be engaged.
Harriet Why, Randall, I had no idea that you were so prudish.
Randall (*stiffly*) I am sorry you should consider me so but I hope you will remember what I have said.
Harriet Very well, Randall. (*Turning away, she sighs*) Only . . .
Randall Only what?
Harriet (*rising*) If our conversation is to be restricted in this fashion, soon all we shall be able to do will be to exchange platitudes on the respective states of our health and the weather.
Randall Really, Harriet, I had no idea that you could be so irresponsible.
Harriet We're learning a good deal about each other today.

Lesley Hallam comes in impulsively by the double door. At twenty-four she is the youngest of the Hallams and is somewhat spoiled in consequence. Lesley still affects the airs of the indulged youngest of the family and this seems less incongruous than it might be because she is still immature. She is quite pretty in an unobtrusive fashion, and she is carrying an envelope in her hand

Lesley (*as she enters*) Harriet . . . (*She pauses when she sees Randall*) Oh, I'm sorry. I didn't know you were still here, Randall. I wouldn't have disturbed you . . .
Randall You're not disturbing us.
Harriet (*with a noticeable lack of warmth*) No, do come in, Lesley.

Lesley closes the door and comes over to them

Did you want me?
Lesley Only to tell you that the post has been and there's a letter from my dear Harry.
Randall But you haven't opened it yet.
Harriet Oh, she never does right away. She always carries his letters about for a while to prolong the enjoyment of reading them.
Lesley But I have to, Randall. I just have to. Dear Harry writes the shortest, dullest letters. Surely, *something* happens worth recording in the life of a regimental adjutant stationed in York.
Randall Garrison duty is very dull, I'm told.
Lesley York is a delightful city but you would never think so from Harry's letters. I know almost exactly what he has written before I tear the envelope. So I put off opening it as long as possible in the hope that, this

time, he's going to surprise me. (*Sadly, she shakes her head*) But he never does.

Randall (*warmly encouraging*) He will. He will surprise you one of these days. You'll see.

Lesley If he would only be original and diverting just for once. It isn't much to ask. Oh, but I'm interrupting you . . .

Randall Not at all. I was just going.

Harriet Going? Aren't you staying to tea?

Randall I can't. I have calls to make—Miss Boyd and old Mrs Turner. There isn't much I can do but they both look forward to a visit.

Harriet Come to tea tomorrow then.

Randall With pleasure but I won't be able to stay long—I'll still have to look in on Mrs Turner.

Harriet's face clouds over

You come with me to see her. She'd appreciate a fresh face.

Harriet Oh, I couldn't possibly. There's always so much to see to between tea and dinner.

Lesley You go, Harriet, and I'll look after things.

Harriet But you always forget something.

Lesley seems about to protest

(*Raising her hand*) All right. I'll leave you and Maggie to manage just this once.

Lesley And we'll manage very well. (*Sitting*) You'll be surprised.

As if seeking somebody, Mildred Drew comes in eagerly by the double door. She is a pleasant-looking girl of twenty. Her eager expression fades when she sees the others and gives place to one of embarrassment

Mildred Oh, good afternoon. Good afternoon, Vicar.

Harriet Hello, Mildred.

Randall Good afternoon, Mildred.

Mildred I'm intruding, I'm afraid.

Randall No, no. I'm just off. (*To Harriet*) I really must be on my way.

Harriet I'll see you out.

Randall precedes her to the double door and opens it. Harriet pauses in the doorway

Stay to tea, Mildred.

Harriet goes out

Randall It's good to see you, Mildred—however briefly.

With a little bow, Randall follows Harriet

Mildred turns eagerly to Lesley as the door closes

Mildred Where's Vivian? Where is he?

Act I

Lesley Not home yet. You know he's seldom home before six.
Mildred But he is home. I saw him walking up your drive. That's why I dashed over just as I was. Well, I did just tidy my hair. Is it very forward of me to hurry over like this the moment I see Vivian?
Lesley Of course it isn't. It's quite understandable. After all, you're practically engaged.
Mildred But that's not the same as being officially engaged. It's three weeks and two days to my birthday. Why do you think Aunt Vashti wants us to wait until my birthday? (*She sits in the armchair*)
Lesley Well, it will be so pleasant to announce your engagement on your birthday. Besides, you'll be out of your teens. You'll be twenty—practically of age. You'll be a much more sober and responsible person.
Mildred Not me—I shall be the same foolish, feckless creature I am at this moment. I never knew time to go so slowly. Is it sinful to wish one's life away?
Lesley Not in your case. It's only three weeks. They'll soon pass.
Mildred No, they won't. I keep thinking that something dreadful might happen between now and then. But it couldn't, could it, Lesley?
Lesley You are silly to go on like this.
Mildred Then I torment myself with the thought that Vivian will discover that I'm an empty, silly person consumed by shyness with no pretence to looks and no gift for conversation.
Lesley Dear Mildred! What a shocking state you're in! (*Surveying her*) You're actually a very pretty girl. You're not at all shy and your conversation is charming.
Mildred (*immensely relieved*) Is it? Is it really? (*Her face clouding again*) But that isn't enough. I want to be witty and brilliant for Vivian's sake.
Lesley Whatever for? Vivian couldn't live up to you if you were.
Mildred Oh yes, he could. Vivian is a particularly brilliant person.
Lesley (*amused*) Is he indeed? I'd never noticed it.
Mildred The main trouble with me is that I haven't much experience.
Lesley It's a common failing in people of your age.
Mildred Don't laugh at me. Help me, please. After all, you're not that much older than I am. Do you think I'll begin to mature when I'm twenty?
Lesley (*teasing*) I doubt it.
Mildred Oh, I do hope so. I'm so conscious of my shortcomings.
Lesley Then don't be. Vivian likes you the way you are.
Mildred Likes me? (*She nods soberly and rises*) Yes, I suppose he does. But he really admires a very different sort of woman. Big, bold, handsome women. (*She wanders to the bay window and stands looking out*) I know. I've seen the way he—kindles when he looks at them.
Lesley They're all like that, my dear. Harry's just the same. (*She turns quickly as the double door opens*)

Vivian Hallam comes in. He is twenty-seven, smartly dressed, good-looking and wears the confidence of a young man with an assured future

Here he is.

Mildred turns, delight expressed in every feature. Vivian walks past Lesley, ignoring her. He pauses and stands smiling at Mildred. Lesley observes them, amused

Lesley (*brightly*) I really can't stay here a moment longer. (*She goes to the double door and looks back at them*) Please don't seek to detain me.

The others give no sign of hearing her

Lesley shrugs and goes out by the double door

Vivian holds out his arms and Mildred runs into his embrace. They kiss

Vivian (*still holding her in his arms*) How long have you been here?
Mildred Only a few minutes. I saw you arrive. Oh, it's good to see you, Vivian.
Vivian (*smiling as he releases her*) Is it? You sound as if you hadn't seen me for months.
Mildred It seems like months since last night. (*She sits in the armchair*) And I was feeling so miserable.
Vivian Why should you? I take that as a poor compliment. Don't you relish the prospect of being engaged to me? (*He smiles down at her*)
Mildred Don't say that even in fun. Only one thing means more to me—and that's being married to you.
Vivian Well, it's only a question of time now.
Mildred But the time goes so very slowly. The days simply drag by and anything might happen.
Vivian What, for instance?
Mildred One of us might die.
Vivian (*laughing*) I don't intend to die and you look reasonably healthy to me.
Mildred Or Aunt Vashti might withdraw her consent.
Vivian That wouldn't change things very much. We could still get married in a year.
Mildred A year? Could you wait a year?
Vivian If I had to.
Mildred (*shaking her head*) I couldn't. I'd just go mad. Why, in that time, you could meet some astonishingly beautiful, clever woman and marry her.
Vivian You're quite beautiful enough for me. (*He goes over to the couch and sits*) And I don't think I'd care to marry a clever woman. She'd find me out too easily.
Mildred Is there something to find out? (*She pauses*) Is there?
Vivian Not now. There was once.
Mildred I knew it. I've always felt that you kept something hidden from me.
Vivian It's all over and done with years ago. I haven't thought of it for ages. (*Noticing her troubled expression*) You're not to worry about it. I assure you there's no need.

Act I

Mildred Then I won't if you tell me not to. But I do think you might . . .
Vivian Yes, I ought to have told you before but I've kept putting it off.
Mildred Tell me . . .
Vivian Not now. It'll keep a little longer.
Mildred Just as you say, Vivian. But I want to hear all about it. I'll remind you.
Vivian I'm sure you will. Come over here. (*He pats the couch*)

She goes and sits beside him

What have you been doing today?
Mildred Nothing very much. This morning I wrote some letters, took the dog for a walk and practised the piano.
Vivian And this afternoon?
Mildred I had my lesson and I was writing in my diary when I saw you.
Vivian Writing in your diary? I never knew you kept one. What on earth do you find to record in it?
Mildred My hopes and fears. The small happenings in my life and the great events.
Vivian Ah yes, the great events. Like taking the dog for a walk.
Mildred You're laughing at me. There are great events in everybody's life.
Vivian Of course there are. (*He takes her hand, leans forward and kisses her lightly. Thereafter, they sit with linked hands*)
Mildred What did you do today?
Vivian Nothing very profitable. I've spent most of the day arguing with the representatives of some Greek merchants about a cargo of dried fruit. It isn't up to sample.
Mildred Dried fruit? You mean currants and raisins?
Vivian That's right.
Mildred Oh, Vivian, how very interesting!
Vivian I don't know that it is. But I realize that I'm lucky. I like our business. It's so varied. That's because we're both importers and exporters. We handle so many commodities that I'll become a Jack-of-all-trades and master of none.
Mildred No you won't. No danger of that. I know what you'll become.
Vivian What's that?
Mildred A very clever importer and exporter.

They laugh

Vivian (*suddenly serious*) There's something we must think about fairly soon.
Mildred What is it, Vivian?
Vivian We'll have to decide on where we're going to live.
Mildred Oh yes! Where?
Vivian Somewhere not too far away. I've got my eye on one or two properties. What do you think of Manningham House?
Mildred (*shocked*) Oh, no!
Vivian Why not?

Mildred It's so big. We'd need so many servants. It would be such an extravagance.

Vivian I can afford it. Don't forget that I am a man of substance. We'll have to put on a decent show.

Mildred (*sighing*) I suppose so. (*She rises*) But Manningham House—I don't see myself . . . (*Disconsolately she wanders to the armchair and then faces him*) I could almost wish that your mother hadn't left you all that money.

Vivian But she did. You'll just have to make the best of me as I am—disgustingly rich.

Mildred I wish we could begin our married life in a little place—not much more than a cottage with just one servant . . .

Vivian There's no reason in the world why we shouldn't have a cottage as well.

Mildred Oh, could we?

Vivian Wherever you like—in the country or at the seaside. Just as you please.

Mildred You mean I can choose?

Vivian Of course. It will be one of my wedding presents to you.

Mildred Oh, Vivian, you are so good to me!

Vivian kisses her

The smaller door flies open and Harriet enters hastily, looking worried

Vivian and Mildred are startled

Harriet I'm sorry to break in like this but I've just made a most disturbing discovery.

Vivian What's the matter?

Harriet It appears that Father ordered Maggie to prepare the guest suite and told her not to say anything to me about it. I wouldn't have known a thing about it if I hadn't happened to take a walk up the side staircase.

Vivian This is rather unusual, isn't it?

Harriet It's more than that—it's most peculiar. I don't like it at all. We ought to have a word together. I've told Lillah to call Lesley.

Mildred I'll be going if you want to talk.

Vivian There's no need.

Harriet If you really wouldn't mind, Mildred.

Mildred Of course not. I do understand.

Vivian Then I'll walk back with you.

Mildred No, no. Harriet needs you here. I'll see you later.

Mildred holds up her cheek to him and he kisses her. Then he goes ahead of her to open the double door. Mildred pauses on the threshold

Mildred Good-bye, Harriet. I do hope everything will be all right.

Harriet (*without conviction*) I'm sure it will be. There's probably quite a simple explanation.

Mildred exits by the double door

Act I

Vivian closes the door and strides impatiently over to Harriet

Vivian Really, Harriet! Why did you drive Mildred away like that? You're making a ridiculous fuss about nothing. Of course there's a simple explanation.
Harriet And I'm sure there isn't. This isn't like Father at all. Something's wrong. I feel it in my bones.
Vivian Sometimes you're worse than childish. I can't, for the life of me, see why you should be so upset.
Harriet Can't you? Can't you, indeed? Surely, as Father's housekeeper, I'm entitled to know when a visitor is coming to stay.
Vivian Yes, I suppose you are. (*He takes out a holder into which he inserts a cigarette which he presently lights. He sits on the couch*)
Harriet I had hoped for a measure of sympathy and understanding. I had forgotten that you don't possess those qualities.

Lesley enters quickly by the double door

Lesley (*as she comes in*) Lillah said you wanted me. What is it?
Harriet Only this—I've discovered that Father has ordered Maggie to prepare the guest suite for a lady visitor and specifically told her not to tell me.
Lesley Oh Harriet. How dreadful!
Vivian (*sitting up*) You didn't say that the visitor was a woman.
Harriet Didn't I? Well, perhaps now you see why I'm so concerned.
Lesley What are you so concerned about?
Harriet (*glancing in exasperation from one to the other*) Am I the only one in this house to be able to see further than the end of my nose? He's anxious that we should have a good opinion of her. Don't you see—he's going to marry again.
Vivian Oh, no! Not the Guv'nor!
Lesley Not at his age.
Harriet (*whirling on her*) What do you mean—his age? Father's only in his early fifties—and he's young for his years. He's a fine-looking man, too.
Vivian She's right, you know. He's a great favourite with the girls. I wonder . . .
Harriet Yes, what?
Vivian It's just that I thought he looked particularly elegant today.
Harriet There, you see!
Vivian And he left the office early this afternoon—that's why I'm home early.
Harriet It all fits together. We're to have a stepmother.
Vivian What are you going to do about it, Harriet—forbid the banns? He's of age, you know. If he wants to, he can get married.
Lesley Yes, and why shouldn't he?
Harriet I'll tell you why. Because I don't want to see some stranger sitting in my mother's place . . . the place I have occupied since her death. I don't want to step down and see an alien creature trying to run this house.
Vivian There's that, of course.

Lesley I'm sorry, Harriet. I hadn't thought of it in that way.
Harriet But I have. There's something else. Suppose there are children of this marriage. That's quite a possibility. They'd have to be educated and provided for.
Vivian Oh, yes . . .
Harriet There'll be less for all of us—a good deal less if this comes about.
Vivian What a very mercenary attitude!
Harriet You can afford to be lofty—thanks to what Mother left you. I'm going to marry a poor man. I hope to have children and I'm thinking of them.

Lesley wanders over to the window and idly glances out

Vivian You're letting your imagination run away with you. All this is only speculation.

Lesley, still looking out of the window, gives a little cry of mingled surprise and alarm

Harriet What is it? What's the matter?
Lesley (*staring transfixed*) It's Father. He's just got out of the carriage. There's a woman inside.
Harriet (*going to the window*) Here, let me look.
Vivian Don't let them see you. (*Incongruously, he tiptoes in the direction of the window but halts some distance away peering vainly from behind his sisters*)
Lesley He's raising his hat.
Harriet The carriage is driving away. (*She pulls Lesley away from the window*) Come away. He might look up. What shall we do? What shall we do?
Vivian The first thing is not to give way and to appear much as usual when he comes in. (*He crushes out his cigarette in an ashtray on the secretaire*)
Harriet I couldn't face him. I couldn't face Father at this moment.
Vivian Of course you can. He's the one who will be feeling embarrassed. We're all together in this. (*He holds out his hand to her*) Come on, Harry, sit down.

Harriet takes his hand and permits him to lead her to the couch where she sits

You too, Lesley. Come on—quickly now. (*He bustles Lesley to the couch*)

Lesley sits beside her sister. Vivian surveys them critically

That's all right. But do try to look less like candidates for the scaffold. (*He strolls over to the secretaire and plants himself in front of it*) I'll do very well here—casual but strategically placed.
Harriet (*with hand to her breast*) My heart. My heart is beating so loudly he's sure to hear.
Vivian Calm yourself. The thing to remember is that Father must be feeling worse than you—he's the one who has to make the explanations.

But Rex Hallam is apparently at his ease when he enters by the double door. He registers mild surprise when he sees Vivian and pauses momentarily at the sight of him. Rex is indeed an elegant, good-looking man who has preserved the vigour of his prime. He glances from face to face smiling quizzically

Rex It's good to see you all at home. (*He goes to the bell-push and presses it*)
Harriet Are you ringing for tea, Father?
Rex No, I am not. Did you want tea?
Harriet Not particularly. But I thought you might want a cup.
Rex Lillah took my hat and stick and I asked her to defer tea for half an hour. Does that suit everybody?

He glances round and they signify agreement

It's just that I have had another idea involving either an indulgence or a delaying tactic. I'm not sure which. (*He considers—then shrugs as he gives up*) Perhaps both.

Lillah comes in by the double door. She is an attractive creature dressed in a parlour-maid's uniform and, although her manner could not be described as impudent, there is a most provocative air about her. Her walk contributes to the general impression—that and the occasional telling glance from under her lashes

Ah, Lillah, do you think you could mix me one of my three-finger whiskies?
Lillah Oh yes, sir.
Rex Then pop into the study and do so. (*He takes a key from his waistcoat pocket*) Here's the key of the decanter.
Lillah (*accepting the key*) Very good, sir.

Lillah turns, and her progress to the double door is watched with interest by both Rex and Vivian. She has almost reached the door when Rex calls

Rex Stay.

Lillah pauses and faces them

Will you join me, Vivian?
Vivian No, thank you, Father.
Rex You're very wise. All right, Lillah. Get along, girl. Make haste. Make haste.

Lillah bobs a curtsey and goes out, but not before she has darted an eloquent glance at Vivian

Yes, you're wise, my boy. One shouldn't drink in the afternoon but I feel the particular need of a stimulant. You're home early today, Vivian.
Vivian I came about four—couldn't make any further headway with Versopolous and decided to call it a day.

Rex You don't owe me any explanations. You're a partner and answerable to no-one. You make your own decisions and they're invariably the right ones. I'm proud of you.
Vivian (*embarrassed*) Thank you, Father.
Rex And most of all I'm proud of the way you carried on the business while I was away at the War. Not many young fellows could have done half as well.
Harriet Did you engage a butler today, Father?
Rex No, Harriet. I did not.
Harriet But I understood . . .
Rex This afternoon I interviewed the three applicants Slater had produced for me and decided that none of them was suitable. Two were so decrepit that it was clear they could not give us reasonable service.
Vivian And the other? What about him?
Rex He, at least, was young and nimble but, unfortunately he had a roving eye. We don't want a repetition of the trouble we had with Fletcher.
Harriet Perhaps the simplest thing would be to get rid of Lillah.
Rex I don't agree. I don't see why a girl should be penalized for her looks.
Harriet It isn't just her looks—it's her manner and—and the way she walks.
Rex Harriet, you're outrageous! I think she walks very nicely. Very nicely indeed.

As if to illustrate his defence of her manner of walking, Lillah returns bearing the glass of whisky on a tray. She undulates towards Rex expressing a demure consciousness that both he and Vivian are regarding her with interest

Rex takes the glass, holds it up to the light, and sips his drink before registering appreciation

Yes. That will do very well. All right, Lillah. Get along.

Lillah exits

Rex watches her departure absently and then turns with a sigh

Let's make ourselves comfortable. Sit down, Vivian.

Vivian turns the chair from the secretaire to face inwards and sits upon it

Sure you're all right there, Vivian?
Vivian Perfectly comfortable, thank you, Father.
Rex It's convenient that we're all together. Most convenient. Because I have something of importance to say to you. (*He sits in the armchair, sips his whisky and surveys them before continuing*) This is going to be difficult and unpleasant for me and I ask you to be patient and forbearing until you have heard me out. Can I rely on you?
Lesley (*eagerly*) Yes! Oh, yes!
Harriet Of course, Father.
Vivian You know you can, Father.

Rex I shall be forced to speak of my married life with your mother. I do so with diffidence and I strive for restraint. In the main, we got along reasonably well but she—she shrank from certain aspects of marriage. She was always delicate and, after Lesley was born, the physical side of our marriage was over. And I was still a young man. (*He glances anxiously from Vivian to his daughters*) But this must be dreadful for you. Am I being too outspoken before my own children? Say at once if you think so. Lesley?
Lesley No, Father.
Rex Harriet?
Harriet (*without encouragement*) Go on if it helps you, Father.

Rex sips his whisky reflectively before continuing

Rex I am anxious not to disturb your memories and yet I must be fair to myself and keep a balance. You see, there I was, in some respects a bachelor, when I met Frances—quite casually. She was from the North—warm-hearted and just about the most attractive woman I ever met. We—we came to an arrangement and we lived together for some years.
Harriet No!
Rex Oh yes, Harriet. I warned you it was going to be difficult. It's difficult for me to tell you and I've no doubt that it's difficult to believe this of your own father. I used to visit Frances when I could and we'd spend holidays and weekends together. We were very happy . . . (*He breaks off suddenly conscious of the glass in his hand*) Vivian.
Vivian Yes, Father.
Rex (*holding out his glass*) This isn't helping me at all. Will you please take it from me?

Vivian comes over, takes the glass and stands looking down at his father

Vivian I'm glad you were happy.
Rex Thank you.
Lesley So am I, Father, So am I.
Rex You are very kind—all of you.

Rex's glance rests pleadingly on Harriet who is regarding him with a severe expression. She does not speak until Vivian has returned to the secretaire and rid himself of the glass

Harriet You say all this was years ago?
Rex (*nodding*) Yes.
Harriet Then what made you suddenly decide to tell us about it?
Rex You'll see why in a moment or two.

Vivian resumes his seat

Your sympathy encourages me to tell you that the time I spent with Frances was the happiest of my whole life. I hope that each of you may find such happiness one day. (*He rises, paces restlessly to the window, looks out briefly, then returns*) Lately, I've been troubled. It seems to me that I've turned my back on the best part of my life. Here, in Medham,

they know me as a one-time soldier, a successful City merchant—the Vicar's Warden at St Thomas's Church. But they do not know that I was the lover of Frances. It is the thing I am most proud of in my life—my greatest achievement and it is high time that I acknowledged it.
Vivian But how? What are you going to do?
Rex I had no idea until a week ago last Sunday when I stood at the altar with the other sidesmen. Then, quite suddenly, I saw that much of my life had been a lie, lived in the shadow. But I realized it wasn't too late. It was still in my power to make some amends to Frances.
Harriet (*harshly, as she rises*) When is she coming here? When are you going to bring her?
Rex (*blankly*) Bring her? What are you talking about?
Harriet This Frances—whatever her name is. When is she coming?
Rex Frances is dead, my dear. She died three years ago.

Lesley and Vivian have now also risen and all three regard him in bewilderment

Vivian Then what do you mean about making amends?
Rex We had a child—a daughter.
Lesley And she's still alive?
Rex Very much so.
Lesley When can we meet her?
Harriet (*impatiently waving her to silence*) Just a minute, Lesley. I'd like to get something settled. (*Turning to Rex*) You mean you want her to come and keep house for you. Is that it, Father?
Rex No, it isn't. (*He rises*) She isn't exactly domesticated and she's younger than all of you. She's only just had her twenty-first birthday. Compared to you, she's a child—a mere child.
Harriet (*ungraciously*) Then why didn't you say so before? (*She turns away*)
Rex (*following her*) What's all this talk of housekeepers, Harriet? Are you weary of the tedium? (*In an attempt to conciliate her, he puts his hand on her arm*) Are you anxious to lay down your burden?
Harriet By no means. (*Withdrawing*) But I still don't understand. Do you mean to bring her here?
Rex I do—and I hope you'll welcome her, if only for my sake.
Harriet In what capacity will she be coming?
Rex I should have thought that would be obvious: as my daughter—my youngest daughter. I mean to acknowledge her.
Harriet Do you realize what it will mean in a place like this? You are the most popular and respected man in Medham. It will be a public scandal.
Rex Possibly. For a little while. But I shall be proclaiming the truth and the truth can't hurt us.
Harriet Can't it? I think you'll find that this particular truth can hurt each one of us in this room. Hurt us irreparably. Have you really thought what this is going to mean to us?
Lesley You're only thinking of yourself, Harriet—only speaking for yourself. After all, this is Father's house. If he wants her here then that is all that matters.

Act I

Lesley and Vivian gravitate towards their father so that the three form a united group, with Harriet moving away to isolate herself

Vivian Of course it is. You're being downright selfish. All three of us are engaged. Presumably, we shall soon be setting up homes of our own. It will be a good thing if this girl is here to keep Father company.

Harriet You take this—this revelation very lightly it seems to me. What did Father say? He was "practically a bachelor" when he met this—this Frances person. Was he? Was he, in any real sense, a bachelor? Our mother was still alive. Could he justify setting aside his marriage vows just because his wife was an invalid? I seem to remember something in the marriage service about cherishing one another in sickness and in health. Surely, there is something in marriage besides what you have described as the physical side.

Rex I wish, Harriet, you'd try to see things a little more from my point of view. I had a good deal to bear. With me, your mother was very far from being an uncomplaining invalid. She was fretful and querulous ...

Harriet I don't know how you can stand there, with her portrait in the room, and speak so slightingly of her and so fondly of this woman who was your mistress. (*She looks up at the portrait*) If she can look down on us what will she think of Lesley and Vivian? Or of you, Father?

Rex If she can look down, she'll think that you're uncharitable. And she'll understand me better than she did in her lifetime. If she understands, she'll forgive me.

Vivian You're doing your best to make this more difficult for Father. This is one occasion when he needs our support.

Lesley Of course he does. He needs all the help and sympathy we can give him.

Harriet So I'm in the minority again? (*She laughs unpleasantly*) I'm getting used to it. Because I understand why. You're both Father's children—easygoing creatures with accommodating consciences. I'm my mother's daughter. And I'm proud of it. (*Proudly, too, she looks up at her mother's portrait. Then she wheels on Rex*) When are we to expect her?

Rex Now. At once.

Harriet You mean she's here? In the house?

Rex Yes. She came with me in the carriage. Baines took her to see the view of the Common. Then he was to return with her and she was to wait with Maggie until we rang. Will you ring, Vivian?

Vivian moves towards the bell-push

Harriet No!

Vivian is checked by Harriet's outcry and they all look at her

I won't have it! I won't have her in here! It's not fair to spring her on us like this and I won't stay here and receive her in my mother's drawing room.

Rex As you will, of course. I would not ask you to do anything which conflicted with your sense of duty. But I shall be deeply offended and bitterly disappointed if you do not stay and receive my youngest daughter. If you please, Vivian.

Vivian goes over and presses the bell-push and then returns to his former position. They are all watching Harriet who now stands irresolute

Harriet It's all so wickedly unfair. To her as well as us. How can you expect a girl with her background and upbringing to feel at home here?

Rex I don't know what kind of girl you are expecting, Harriet, but she was educated at a good boarding school and finished in Switzerland. I felt I owed her that.

Harriet (*tartly*) It's reassuring to know that she has enjoyed all the advantages.

Vivian What's her name?

Rex She took the name of Ollerenshaw—the name of the man Frances eventually married. He's on the music halls.

Harriet (*faintly*) The music halls!

Rex Her Christian name is Nicola.

Vivian Nicola—a pretty name.

The double door opens and Maggie enters to announce

Maggie The young lady, sir.

Nicola enters. She is decidedly attractive, completely self-possessed, and her clothes are an adornment worn with an eye for effect. The other young women appear drab in comparison with her. Smiling, she surveys them from the threshold. Her appraisal is not long but it is penetrating. Already she knows more about the Hallams than they do about her. Maggie withdraws

Nicola (*turning to Rex*) But they're just like their photographs! They're exactly as I expected to find them! You needn't introduce us. (*Impulsively, hands extended, she runs over to Harriet*) I hope we're going to be great friends, Harriet.

Nicola seizes Harriet's hands and plants a kiss on her impassive cheek. Apparently undisturbed by the coolness of Harriet's reception, she goes, in the same eager fashion to Lesley who returns her kiss. The two girls stand smiling at each other

Lesley I know we shall be friends, Nicola.

Nicola Of course we shall.

More deliberately, Nicola goes over to Vivian who prepares to kiss her. Nicola, however, demurely holds out her hand to him and, disappointedly, he takes it

I'm very glad to meet you at last, Vivian.

Vivian (*retaining her hand as she seeks to withdraw it and covering it with his other hand*) I cannot say that you are as I expected because I've only just learned of your existence. But I could not have imagined a more delightful relative.

Act I

Nicola (*withdrawing her hand and turning to Rex*) There! Isn't that gallant?

Nicola goes and stands beside Rex, still smiling round at them. Harriet alone remains unresponsive

It's curious but I don't feel a bit as if I'm meeting you for the first time.
Rex We're very happy to have you, my dear.
Nicola And I'm happy to be here. (*She suddenly looks at Harriet and her glance becomes fixed*) Harriet isn't happy that I'm here though. (*Quickly, she checks a movement of protest from Rex with a raised hand*) I should feel just the same if I'd had an unknown relative thrust upon me—especially one who can hardly be considered respectable. Don't let it trouble you. Or any of us. (*Smiling directly at Harriet*) We shall get on all right, Harriet, once the strangeness has worn off.
Rex This has been rather a shock to Harriet. But we'll all settle down presently. We'll have tea in a few minutes but first I thought you'd like to see your suite.
Nicola Suite? Surely you mean my room?
Rex No, no. That's my surprise. We have a guest suite with its own private staircase through there (*indicating the small door*) and it is to be yours. You can be gregarious or withdrawn as the fancy dictates. Vivian and I have our studies and both the girls have their own sitting rooms. This drawing-room is common ground.
Nicola It sounds an excellent arrangement.
Rex The only thing is that sometimes one comes in here prepared to be gregarious and finds that everybody else is being private in their various apartments. But it works very well in the main.
Nicola I'm sure it does. And now, I'd love to see my suite. (*She moves to go, but checks when she sees Harriet is pointedly turned away*)

Rex glances entreatingly at Harriet, but she remains unresponsive

Rex Very well, then. Come with me.

Rex goes to the small door, opens it and looks back in surprise when he sees that Nicola has made no attempt to follow him. Instead, she is looking from one to the other of the Hallams with a speculative, not very pleasant, smile

What's the matter?
Nicola I was just looking at you all. You're a family. I'm an individual. Some might see me as a lonely person and pity me. They would be quite wrong to do so. For I have had experience of families before now and they are seldom what they seem. At first glance they look as you do—united and easy with each other. When you get to know them better, you find that they live as strangers who cannot talk to each other about anything important. They are people linked together by accident of birth, lonelier and more troubled than those who live alone. I look at you all and I wonder . . .
Rex You needn't. We're tolerant of one another, we're sympathetic and you'll find we understand one another reasonably well.

Nicola Perhaps I will—(*she looks pointedly at Harriet*)—if I stay long enough. (*She walks to the door and pauses in front of Rex as she looks back at them*) Or I might find you're like all the other families but just a little better at hiding from one another. We'll see.

Smiling, Nicola nods to them and goes out. Rex expresses mild bewilderment, shrugs indulgently and follows Nicola, closing the door behind them. The other three stand staring at the closed door

Harriet Father is quite wrong about her. She isn't a child at all.

CURTAIN

SCENE 2

The same. Late on Friday evening

The curtains are drawn and the gas chandelier is lit and spreading its brightest glow in the area surrounding the couch. Nicola, obviously bored, is seated in the armchair leafing through a magazine. Lesley is sitting on the couch engaged with some embroidery. Harriet is busy with her account books and bills at the secretaire. Nicola looks round the room, seeking some diversion. She finds none and her gaze comes to rest on Harriet and Lesley. Sighing petulantly, she closes the magazine

Nicola Is it always as lively as this in the evenings?
Harriet (*annoyed at being interrupted in her addition*) Oh! (*Irritated, she turns round*) What did you say?
Nicola I asked if it was always as lively as this in the evenings.
Harriet Doubtless, you intend to be sarcastic. This is not, I am afraid, a particularly enlivening evening and I am sorry you lack the resources to entertain yourself. I am busy, as you see, with my accounts. As for Lesley and myself, we often enjoy a quiet evening like this. It provides one with an interval for reflection.
Nicola Oh, does it? (*She rises and wanders in the direction of the window*) Everybody to their taste. (*She yawns and stretches—actions noted by Harriet with disapproval*) I have a very different idea of enjoyment.
Harriet (*grimly*) I feel quite certain you have.

Harriet and Nicola exchange a long, hard stare. An atmosphere is developing. Lesley hastens to avert a clash

Lesley It isn't always like this, Nicola. We have our excitements. We have our At Home days, we give tea and dinner parties and we go to parties given by our friends. Then there are lectures and concerts . . .
Harriet But these, I am sure, would seem dull affairs to you.
Nicola Much depends, of course, on the company present on these occasions.
Lesley (*hastily interposing*) Then we have family outings to the theatre. An outing is quite an event. Father books a table at a restaurant—always a fashionable place—and then we go to the theatre. Father is

Act I

invariably most amusing in the restaurant and very interesting when he comments on the performance afterwards.

Nicola It all sounds most diverting.

Lesley Oh, and I almost forgot. We have musical evenings when everybody plays and sings.

Nicola (*kindling*) I like a good sing-song myself

Harriet (*acidly*) This isn't that sort of entertainment. We take our music seriously in Medham.

Nicola I know just what you mean—I've had some. Personally, I've always believed that music was intended to be enjoyed—not suffered. (*Petulantly she returns to her chair*)

Lesley (*after a brief, charged silence*) What do you mean by a sing-song?

Nicola (*increasingly animated*) Well, I think it's about the jolliest way of passing the time. (*She rises and once more crosses to Lesley*) Every so often, friends of Joe's come round to our place. They're all pro's, of course. (*She breaks off and eyes them suspiciously*) You did know that Joe was on the halls?

Lesley Oh, yes. Father told us.

Harriet Yes. We had been told.

Harriet's tone suggests that Joe is guilty of something not far removed from a capital crime. Nicola gives Harriet a sharp glance but her enthusiasm revives as she continues

Nicola Everybody does something—one after the other. It doesn't matter what. Singing, dancing, conjuring or doing impersonations. The piano is tinkling away like mad all the time. You can't keep your toes from tapping in time to the music. You never know what's coming next. That's the marvellous, the exciting thing you never know. Oh, it's the greatest fun in the world. You wouldn't get a better bill at the Palace than we have right in our drawing room.

Harriet And they are all professional people who do this for a living?

Nicola That's right. All pro's. I told you. They're the people who make the music that gets right inside you until it echoes in your brain and bubbles in your blood. They're the people who *live* music.

Lesley And what do you do, Nicola? What do you do when its your turn?

Nicola Whatever comes into my head—sing, dance or do impersonations.

Harriet You must be singularly versatile.

Nicola (*suddenly bleak*) You'd be surprised how versatile.

Lesley Perhaps you'll go on the halls.

Nicola Perhaps. (*Reacting to Lesley's obvious interest*) You ought to hear some of the comedians when they know they can really let themselves go. You never heard anything like it.

Harriet I'm sure I haven't—and I don't think I want to.

Nicola Maybe you're right. I've always said that Dan Markham could make a cat laugh. (*She studies Harriet's unsmiling face*) Since I've met you, I've had reason to change my mind.

Harriet (*rising menacingly*) Are you trying to be insulting?

Nicola Not yet, darling. Not yet. When I try to be insulting I leave nobody in any doubt as to my intentions. But you've been offensive to me and I always believe in giving as good as I get.

Harriet and Nicola glare at each other for a moment. Then, still glaring fixedly at Harriet, Nicola moves slowly and purposefully over to her. Lesley watches tensely, frozen with apprehension. In spite of herself, Harriet is increasingly intimidated as Nicola approaches. Nicola halts before Harriet and, when she speaks, her tone is surprisingly conciliatory

Let's stop, shall we? We're embarrassing Lesley.

Harriet Stop by all means since you began it.

Lesley I *was* embarrassed. I don't like arguments. Arguments lead to quarrels and quarrels distress me very much.

Nicola (*with her eyes on Harriet*) They don't bother me. Quarrels—arguments—they're all in a lifetime. But we'll not quarrel, Lesley. I should hate to distress you.

Nicola returns to her chair and perches inelegantly on the edge of it. Irritated, Harriet watches her. She opens her mouth to issue a rebuke but, catching Nicola's eye, thinks better of it. Desperately, she seeks a change of subject. She rises and goes over to Lesley

Harriet What news had you from Harry today?

Lesley Oh, dear! I forgot! I haven't opened his letter. (*She reaches for her reticule and takes the letter from it*) It isn't that I don't love him dearly but I know just what is in the envelope.

An expression of mischief lights up Lesley's face. She offers the letter to Nicola who accepts it

Here, you take it, Nicola. Open it and read it to yourself. I'll guess what's in it and you tell me whether I'm right.

Harriet (*shocked*) Oh, no! You mustn't do that, Lesley.

Lesley Why ever not? There's never anything in Harry's letters that anybody might not read. (*Her face clouding.*) Unfortunately.

Harriet Just the same, you ought not to let other people read his letters.

Lesley Don't be silly, Harriet. It can't do any harm. Besides, Nicola isn't other people—she's one of the family. (*To Nicola*) Have you read it?

Nicola Yes, It's quite short.

Lesley Right, then. Almost certainly, he opens with a comment about the weather.

Nicola (*reading, and imitating throughout, with some success, a "military" voice*) "It's been raining steadily here for the past twenty-four hours. Hope it is keeping fine with you."

Lesley There! Then there will be a mention of some military activity. (*She laughs uproariously at Nicola's reading*)

Nicola (*rising and burlesquing the march and rubbing with embrocation*) "We did a fifteen-mile route march the day before yesterday. It did us a power of good. I was a bit stiff afterwards but a good rub with embrocation put me right."

Lesley For Harry that's quite a piece of sustained narrative. Now he'll begin to run out of inspiration, so he'll refer to his prospect of leave and limp to a conclusion.

Nicola sits again in the armchair and accompanies the rest of the reading with extravagant gestures

Nicola "There's a good chance that I'll get some leave next month when, needless to say, I shall lose no time in speeding southwards. I look forward to seeing you. Until then, all my love. Yours, as always, affectionately, Harry." (*She looks up*) Then there are two kisses.

Lesley Not really? (*She snatches the letter and inspects it*) So there are. Quite a departure.

Nicola You really were astonishingly accurate.

Lesley It wasn't difficult. If you've read one of Harry's letters, you've read the lot.

Harriet (*rising*) I think you've behaved abominably—both of you! What would Harry say if he knew you passed his letters around and made fun of them?

Nicola Since he won't know, it isn't likely to hurt him.

Harriet That is the worst possible defence. (*She gathers her bills together, slips them into her book and slams it shut*) If you don't mind, I'll finish my accounts in my room.

Nicola Don't let me drive you away.

Harriet has started for the double door but pauses now and whirls to face Nicola

Harriet Rest assured—I won't let you do that.

Harriet goes out. Nicola watches her departure and then, with a mirthless laugh, turns to Lesley

Nicola My charm seems wasted on Harriet.

Lesley You do rather rub her up the wrong way.

Nicola It'll do her good for a change. Anyway, she asked for it. She makes it plain that she doesn't like me.

Lesley You must make allowances. She was very close to our mother.

Nicola And my very existence is a reproach to her mother's memory—is that it?

Lesley Give her time. She'll get over it.

Nicola I wouldn't bet on it. Will you tell her something from me? Tell her if she fights me she'll get hurt. Tell her, too, that she's bound to lose. I've been fighting for most of my life and I usually win because I don't hamper myself by keeping to the rules. If Harriet's wise, she'll leave me alone. You'll tell her?

Lesley If you think it wise. I wouldn't like there to be any real trouble between you.

Nicola There won't be—if she's sensible. (*She looks round the room seeking distraction. The room defeats her*) Now what shall we do?

Lesley Well, I had thought of going to bed.

Nicola But you went to bed early last night, too! Why, it's scarcely half-past ten.
Lesley It's almost a quarter to eleven and we're usually in bed by a little after ten.
Nicola (*incredulously*) Are you really?
Lesley Of course Father and Vivian often stay out very late.
Nicola As late as eleven o'clock?
Lesley Oh, sometimes much later. (*Realizing*) You're making fun of me.
Nicola (*laughing*) Just a bit. I couldn't resist it. (*She goes to the settee and sits beside Lesley*)
Lesley Are we so deadly dull, Nicola?
Nicola Not at all. I find you all most interesting. (*Studying her carefully*) Perhaps if I were to take you in hand a little . . .
Lesley Oh, I wish you would! I'm sure you could teach me a great deal. Since you came, I've been so dissatisfied with myself—with my hair—my clothes—the way I walk.
Nicola You're very sweet as you are. Now run along and get your beauty sleep.
Lesley But I don't like leaving you by yourself.
Nicola Oh, I'll read a little and then come up. Another early night won't do me any lasting harm.
Lesley If you're sure you'll be all right . . .
Nicola As right as rain. Get off with you.
Lesley Good night, Nicola, dear. (*She kisses her on the cheek*)

Nicola looks surprised

Nicola Good night, Lesley.

Lesley gathers up her embroidery and goes towards the double door. She pauses there when Nicola speaks

Don't forget to tell Harriet what I said.
Lesley I'll tell her. Good night.

Lesley goes

Nicola touches her cheek where Lesley kissed it, then sits and tries to read her magazine. She soon abandons it and, with a sigh of exasperation, casts it aside, rises and begins to prowl round the room

Lillah enters with a whisky decanter, soda-water syphon and glasses on a tray. She is surprised when she sees Nicola

Nicola Not yet. I'm not really an early bird. (*She inspects the tray*) What have you got there?
Lillah The master's whisky. He likes a nightcap when he comes in.
Nicola But why are there two glasses?
Lillah (*rather taken aback*) Sometimes Mr Vivian has a drink before retiring. You don't miss much.
Nicola No. I keep my eyes open.

Nicola sits again in the armchair. Lillah places the tray on the secretaire

Do you like it here, Lillah?
Lillah It's not bad, miss. Some might describe this as a good situation. But I don't think I was cut out for domestic service. (*Her hand goes up to her hair and she preens herself*) It's not what I care for.
Nicola Oh? What do you think you'd like to do?
Lillah Well, what I'd really like . . . (*She breaks off and looks entreatingly at Nicola*) You won't laugh at me, miss? (*She moves, with her swaying walk, in front of the table*)
Nicola No, no. Of course not.
Lillah I'd really like to live the life of a lady. I'd like lovely clothes and a nice house with servants to wait on me for a change. I'd like to have my tea from a silver service every afternoon and have a dressing table covered with pots of cream and bottles of scent. (*She looks wistful and sighs*) Trouble is, you've got to find a man to provide all that. And when you've found one, what have you got? Mind you, if I found one of the right sort, I wouldn't be too fussy about marriage.
Nicola With your looks, Lillah, you shouldn't have any difficulty.
Lillah If I wasn't a servant, I'd manage it easy. But men don't like to take up with a servant—they think it lowers them. Not that they mind a bit of nonsense on the sly. Oh, yes. You've got to watch them, I can tell you! But, even if they get a servant in the family way, they never marry her. The most they do is get the baby adopted and help the girl to a new situation. And that's not much good to a girl, is it?
Nicola No, it isn't. You've a very realistic point of view.
Lillah I've got to have. You won't say a word to Miss Harriet, will you, miss?
Nicola Not a word, I promise you.
Lillah Only I felt I could talk to you. Thank you. Good night, miss. (*She curtsies briefly and turns to go*)
Nicola Lillah.
Lillah (*pausing at the double door*) Yes, miss?
Nicola I met Fletcher.
Lillah (*returning and looking disturbed*) Fletcher, miss? When? When was this?
Nicola Never mind. It was quite by accident. He didn't know who I was. Naturally, I was interested when I learned he had been butler here. I encouraged him to talk. He told me—everything.
Lillah But you haven't said anything to anybody here, have you? Not to any of them? I couldn't bear it if you had.
Nicola (*reassuring*) Of course I haven't. But meeting Fletcher decided me to accept Colonel Hallam's invitation. It seemed to me that this must be an interesting household. It is, too. (*She smiles at Lillah and pats her shoulder*). Don't look so worried. I'm your friend. I'm on your side.
Lillah (*with an attempt at an answering smile*) Thank you, miss. I'll go now if you'll excuse me. (*But she hesitates*) How was Fletcher, miss?
Nicola Well enough, I suppose. But angry—resentful and bitter.
Lillah He would be. But what could he do? He's only a servant, after all.

Maggie comes in by the double door. Her glance ranges from Lillah to Nicola and back to Lillah

Maggie Excuse me, miss. You can go to bed if you've finished, Lillah.
Lillah I was just going, Mrs Walters. Good night, miss.

Lillah goes

Maggie Can I get you anything, miss?
Nicola No, thank you.
Maggie You don't want to encourage Lillah, miss. She's a great talker.
Nicola You needn't worry, Maggie. She didn't tell me anything I didn't know already. I met Fletcher before I came here.
Maggie I see, miss. Are you here to make trouble?
Nicola To make trouble? (*She laughs*) That would depend on the way things turn out. You don't like having me here, do you, Maggie?
Maggie That's not for me to say, miss.
Nicola Which means you don't. How long have you been with the family?
Maggie Just short of twenty years, miss. The late mistress engaged me.
Nicola Suppose I were to make this my home? You'd have to change your tune, wouldn't you?
Maggie Perhaps, miss. Or find a new situation.
Nicola Which wouldn't be easy at your age.
Maggie That's something I'd have to find out, miss. Will that be all?
Nicola Just about. I've enjoyed our little chat, Maggie.

Maggie goes out

Nicola looks reflective when she has gone. Then she notices the whisky and crosses to it. She pours a stiff whisky, adds a little soda and swallows the drink in two or three gulps. Quickly, she replenishes her glass, carries it over to the couch and settles herself comfortably and sips her drink

> *Rex enters with the air of a man who has spent a convivial evening at his club. He is wearing hat, light overcoat and gloves when he comes in. He is surprised to see Nicola and removes his hat with a flourish*

Rex Well, now. I didn't expect to find you still up at this hour.
Nicola I'm used to a later bedtime than most people in this house.

Rex begins to remove coat and gloves, distributing them with his hat neatly on the chair by the secretaire

Rex Know what they called you at the club tonight? My daughter of the left hand. That's what they called you.
Nicola I can just imagine. In an atmosphere of knowing nods and alcoholic sentimentality.
Rex You're altogether too hard on them. They're excellent fellows. Excellent. (*He now notices the glass in her hand*) What are you drinking? Not whisky, is it?
Nicola I won't commit myself but it did come out of that decanter over there.

Rex (*laughing*) Did it now? Did it indeed? What next? What next, I wonder? (*He stops laughing and is suddenly grave*) Mark you, Frances didn't object to a glass now and then. In fact, she liked a drink. And who's to blame her?

Nicola Exactly. What's sauce for the goose . . .

Rex (*exitedly*) But that's it! That's what she used to say! You must have learned it from her. (*Inclining towards her with exaggerated courtesy*) Do you mind if I join you?

Nicola (*with an extravagant gesture of assent*) Please do.

He goes to the secretaire, pours whisky into his glass and, impulsively, turns to her

Rex May I get you another?

For answer, she drains her glass and offers it. He comes over and takes it, chuckling as he returns to the secretaire. With the decanter poised, he looks at her

How do you like it—weak or strong?

Nicola There's only one way to drink whisky. Make mine strong.

He complies, squirts a little soda in each glass and comes across to the couch with the drinks. He hands Nicola her glass, settles himself beside her and regards her benignly

Rex Well, this is very pleasant. (*His expression changes as he watches her drink her whisky*) Though I'm sure it's wrong for you to be sitting here drinking whisky at this time of night.

Nicola Have you ever noticed how many things are both pleasant and wrong?

Rex You're absolutely right! You've got to make up your mind to compromise if you're going to get any enjoyment at all.

Nicola I made up my mind long ago. We're here only a short time and it's up to us to make the best of it while we can.

Rex I entirely agree! You're lucky to have discovered it so soon. I only found out when I met your mother.

Nicola Where did you meet her?

Rex But, surely, you know?

Nicola I don't know whether I do or not. She told me several versions. She was inclined to—improve stories.

Rex (*laughing*) She most certainly was! Well, we encountered one another on Victoria Station.

Nicola She told me it was in a restaurant.

Rex There! You see? She was having difficulty in finding a porter. I found her one and helped her to a cab. Somehow, I found myself inside the cab. Unaccountably, we had dinner together and then . . .

Nicola Quite incredibly, you found you had set up house together at St John's Wood.

Rex Yes, but by then I knew what was happening. We were experiencing the greatest happiness possible to human beings. And we did harm to nobody—unless it was you. Do you mind that we were happy at your expense?

Nicola Not in the least. I'm all right.

Rex Of course you are. One has only to look at you—listen to you—watch you move. You're all right. (*He raises his empty glass*) Let's drink to it. (*He makes two attempts to rise and does so after he has heaved himself upright*)

Nicola No more for me.

Rex (*looking at her reprovingly*) Nonsense. Must have one more. Special occasion. (*He starts for the secretaire, corrects a tendency to lurch but trips and staggers just short of his objective. Chuckling, he turns to Nicola*) See that? Means I'm getting whiffled. Have to go carefully. (*And he does for the rest of the journey*)

Nicola (*watching him apprehensively*) I don't think we ought to have any more—either of us.

Rex (*busily pouring*) Just this one. Just a final nightcap. It'll help you to sleep.

Nicola I don't need any help. I go to sleep as soon as my head touches the pillow.

Rex Then you're very lucky. Have this one to keep me company. (*He squirts a little soda into each of two large whiskies*) There we are. (*Moving with studied care, he makes the return journey to the couch without incident and hands the glass to Nicola. He sits beside her*) We were going to drink to something. Oh, yes. You're all right, Nicola. That's it. (*He raises his glass*) Here's to you. (*He drinks*)

Nicola Thank you. (*She raises her glass and sips*)

Rex But are you really all right? Are you settling down?

Nicola As well as can be expected in the circumstances.

Rex What circum—circumstances?

Nicola Harriet.

Rex Is she being difficult?

Nicola When she's not being impossible.

Rex She'll get over it.

Nicola Not her. She's enjoyed being your housekeeper for too long and she sees me as an intruder. A bastard intruder, moreover.

Rex Did she say that? Because if she did—

Nicola She doesn't have to. It's implied in her manner. She doesn't want me here and nothing will change her. If I lived here a lifetime, she'd never be reconciled to the idea.

Rex Very well, then. Very well. (*He rises with an air of resolution*) Let her be the one to go.

Nicola Don't be ridiculous! This is her home.

Rex Oh, I'm not going to turn her out or ask her to leave. Nothing like that. (*He grins craftily and takes a drink*) I'll just make it easy for her to go.

Nicola Easy for her? I don't understand.

Rex She's engaged to the Vicar. You'll meet him. Between ourselves, I don't think he's very keen to get married. Can't say I blame him. Harriet's a bit formidable. But, if I settle a good round sum on them, there'll be an end of his excuses and he'll lead Harriet to the altar.
Nicola But who'd keep house for you when she's gone?
Rex You would, of course. (*He drains his glass and smiles at her*)
Nicola You'd lose a good deal by the exchange. She's very competent. I've no experience of running a place like this.
Rex You've kept house for Ollerenshaw.
Nicola A very different establishment. A haphazard, bohemian household. Besides, I had a professional housekeeper to help me.
Rex You'd have one here. Maggie would be your lieutenant.
Nicola She wouldn't stay if Harriet went. (*She is sipping her drink reflectively as if considering the prospect*)
Rex The girls are both engaged and Vivian's engagement will be announced in a week or so. (*He comes over and sits beside her*) In a year or so they'll all be gone.
Nicola And you'll make it easier for the others to get married?
Rex It won't be necessary in Vivian's case.
Nicola Why not?
Rex His mother was an heiress. She left only relatively small sums to me and the girls. The bulk of her fortune went to Vivian. He's a very wealthy young man.
Nicola (*clearly impressed*) Is he now? (*She rises, thoughtfully and reflectively circles the table*) How very interesting.
Rex It hasn't spoiled him, though. He works very hard. Kept the business going when I was away at the War.
Nicola He's the one who counts with you, isn't he?
Rex Vivian's a fine fellow. All my good qualities and none of my vices. I think the world of him. The girls are all right . . . But you're worth the pair of them.
Nicola What a stupid thing to say! (*She moves up to the window*) You really know nothing of me. I'd hate it here. I'd stifle among these stockbrokers and merchants and their wives. All these large houses with their well-kept lawns and their servants. All this stuffiness and smothering respectability. And the women! They're the worst of all! Looking down their noses and trying to queen it over one another. (*Suddenly venomous*) I'd like to tell them that their husbands don't love them and that they keep mistresses in Chelsea and Bloomsbury. Just to see their faces! Just to see them!
Rex Don't talk like that. You can't possibly mean what you say. In time, you'd grow to like it here.
Nicola If I thought there was any danger of that, I'd kill myself. No. I know what's the matter with me. I don't like people—except my own sort. They're few enough, it seems. I loathe and despise the fat-witted creatures who live round here.
Rex Very well, then. We shall have only your sort of people to visit us.
Nicola You mean Joe Ollerenshaw and his crowd?

Rex If you really want them.
Nicola You're making it sound very attractive.
Rex I mean to. It means everything to me.
Nicola Now you're exaggerating.
Rex No, I'm not. Come and sit down.

Obediently, she comes over and sits beside him

Now I want the others to go. The sooner the better. I want us to be here together—just like the old days.
Nicola The old days? I don't know what you're talking about.
Rex I mean when Frances and I lived together. You're so like she was when we first met. So like that sometimes it seems I'm talking to Frances. (*He seizes her hands*) You've got to stay with me! You must! You must!
Nicola (*struggling*) Let go of my hands! You're hurting me!
Rex Not until you promise to stay.

She struggles fiercely but unavailingly. Suddenly, he releases her and, taking her in his arms, kisses her violently. She wrestles desperately and eventually tears herself free, away from the couch. Her arm is raised to fend him off as she shouts piercingly

Nicola Stay where you are! Don't touch me! Don't touch me!

He springs up from the couch, seizes her and kisses her again. They struggle together

The double door flies open and Harriet rushes in. Astonished, she stands holding the door handle

Rex hears the opening door and releases Nicola, who stands panting and glaring

Nicola Please understand that I am in no way responsible for what you have just seen. Your father can, perhaps, explain. I can't—unless he is either mad or drunk.

Nicola turns abruptly, thrusts Rex aside and goes out quickly by the small door

Harriet closes the double door. Rex stands with his face averted. Harriet moves towards him like a person in a waking nightmare

Harriet This is terrible, Father. Terrible for me. And what if Lesley had come in just now? (*She peers at him*) Is she right? Are you drunk?
Rex I've had a drink or two. But that has nothing to do with it.
Harriet Then how could you? Your own daughter! It's horrible . . . . Of course, she can't stay here after this.
Rex She most certainly can! Don't start interfering or you'll be sorry. If you're wise, you won't mention this to anybody. I assure you nothing of the sort will happen again.
Harriet I'll never forget it. I'll never forget seeing you both as I came in.
Rex I'm not going to discuss this with you. There's no reason why I should.

Harriet There's every reason! Do you think I can live in this house knowing that you and she . . .
Rex (*thundering*) Be quiet! Go to bed! Go to bed at once!
Harriet Very well. (*She starts for the double door but pauses to look back at him*) What a pity you can't order me to sleep because I don't think I shall.

Harriet goes out

Rex puts his hand to his head as if to soothe away a sudden ache. He goes to the secretaire, pours a drink and swallows half of it at a gulp. Guiltily, he looks towards the double doors, then shrugs away the idea of Harriet

He finishes the drink, puts down the glass and, with an air of resolution, goes out by the small door

CURTAIN

ACT II

Scene 1

The same. Saturday morning

Sunlight streams in through the window. Vivian is seated in the armchair watching Harriet, who is pacing up and down agitatedly

Vivian You mean they were actually embracing?
Harriet (*halting*) I tell you she was in his arms and he was kissing her passionately. She *appeared* to be struggling.
Vivian Good Lord! How disgusting!
Harriet It was monstrous! Monstrous! I never slept a wink last night. Every time I closed my eyes, I saw them. Oh, it was horrible.
Vivian It wouldn't do any good if I talked to him. He wouldn't listen. You said yourself that he shouted you down.
Harriet Oh, I realize that. It would do more harm than good.
Vivian Well, then . . .
Harriet That girl is up to something. In spite of her outraged behaviour, I shouldn't be surprised if she provoked Father into—into doing what he did.
Vivian Oh come, Harriet!
Harriet Remember that her mother was no better than she ought to have been. And she's been living among low-class music hall performers—and you know what they are.
Vivian No, I don't. What are they?
Harriet Don't be exasperating! I'm trying to save Father from a real danger. And what about Lesley?
Vivian Good Heavens, yes! What can we do?
Harriet Get that girl out of here.
Vivian How can we?
Harriet Show Father what she's really like. (*Going close to him*) Make up to her yourself.
Vivian (*rising*) Me? Don't be silly! She'd box my ears.
Harriet I don't think she would. I think you'd find her responsive. But, even if she did, there'd be a disturbance. She'd tell Father. He'd see how dangerous she is and get rid of her.
Vivian (*considering as he walks away from her*) It might work. Yes, it might. Father would be bound to disapprove . . .
Harriet You'll do it?
Vivian I'll have a shot at it.
Harriet Then take the first chance you get.
Vivian It's surely not that desperate. (*He sits on the couch*)
Harriet It's worse with every night she stays in this house. (*Moving closer*) I'll tell you something about her.

Act II

Vivian Yes?
Harriet Promise not to tell Lesley?
Vivian I promise.
Harriet (*lowering her voice impressively*) She puts stuff on her face.
Vivian (*struggling to hide his amusement*) Does she really?

Nicola enters by the double door

Harriet glances eloquently at Vivian. Nicola regards them suspiciously. Vivian rises

Nicola You're silent. Suddenly silent. That means you were talking about me.
Harriet (*indignantly*) We were not! You may find it hard to believe but there are other, more interesting, topics of conversation.
Nicola (*as she saunters into the room*) You keep your opinion, Harriet. I'll hold fast to mine. (*She surveys Harriet*) I didn't see you at breakfast.
Harriet I was up early. (*Insincerely solicitious*) I trust you passed a restful night.
Nicola I managed to sleep—eventually, thank you.
Harriet I'm so glad. Excuse me. I have a lot to do this morning.

Harriet goes out

Amused, Nicola watches her departure

Nicola She doesn't like me a bit. What a pity! I could grow quite fond of her—in the way one gets used to nasty medicine.
Vivian You mean Harriet is nasty medicine?
Nicola That's your suggestion—not mine. But you know her better than I do.
Vivian Everybody else likes you. You don't have to worry about Harriet's opinion.
Nicola Believe me, I don't. "Everybody" likes me. You mean you do?
Vivian Very much. (*He moves closer to her*) I've been seeking an opportunity to tell you so.
Nicola And now you've told me. There! (*She pats him briefly*) It wasn't very difficult, was it? (*And she turns away from him*)
Vivian Not at all difficult.

He grabs her, turns her roughly to face him and kisses her. When he releases her, she stays in his arms and regards him critically

Nicola You're either not very good at kissing or your heart wasn't in it.

She pulls him to her and kisses him. His arms go closely about her and the kiss becomes increasingly passionate. At length, they separate and Vivian looks at her with the expression of a man who has experienced a revelation

That's better. All you need is practice.

He moves to embrace her again but she fends him off, steps nimbly back, and backs towards the window

Oh, no! That's enough for now. Somebody will come in.

Vivian (*following her*) Then when can I see you again?
Nicola (*evading him*) Oh, I'll be about all day. Just keep your eyes open.
Vivian You know very well what I mean. When can I see you alone?
Nicola You really want to?
Vivian Very much.
Nicola Tonight would be as good a time as any, don't you think?
Vivian Where?
Nicola My suite. When the others have gone to bed.
Vivian Will it—will it be all right?
Nicola It's hard to say. You never know how these things will work out. (*More lightly*) But the encounter promises to be interesting for me and should be instructive for you.
Vivian Don't laugh at me! Don't laugh at me, Nicola! (*He rushes at her and takes her in his arms again*)

> *The kiss threatens to be more protracted than the previous one but the double door flies open and Mildred enters precipitately. She is smiling happily when she comes in but, when she sees them, the smile gives place to an expression of horror and incredulity. She cries out and they move apart. She stares at them for a moment and then, sobbing, runs out closing the door noisily behind her*

Nicola Was that . . .?
Vivian That was her. That was Mildred. They must have returned this morning.
Nicola How very awkward! I told you somebody would come in. What are you going to do now?
Vivian About her? I don't know. I can't think.
Nicola Then you'd better start thinking at once and make it something convincing.
Vivian If you weren't here, I should still hear your voice. If I closed my eyes, I would still see your face. I'd never convince Mildred that I didn't mean it when I kissed you.

He tries to kiss her again but she pushes him away

Nicola Then you'd better try. Go and catch her before she sees one of the others.

> *Vivian is hesitating when Maggie ushers in Randall by the double door. Randall looks troubled and apprehensive*

Maggie If you'll just wait in here, sir . . .

Maggie withdraws

There is a silence which becomes insupportable

Vivian (*moving towards the door*) I'll tell Harriet you're here.
Randall (*catching him by the arm and detaining him*) Please don't! Please don't tell her! It was your father I came to see.

Act II 35

Vivian Oh, very well.

Vivian goes out

Randall is embarrassed at being left alone with Nicola and tries to avoid her eye but she continues to regard him with such a hostile and unflinching stare that he is forced to be the first to speak

Randall I'm afraid Vivian assumed that we had met. My name is Cooper—Randall Cooper.

Nicola There is no need for an introduction. I know who you are and you know who I am. (*She shifts her position slightly to survey him more critically*) Why are you so agitated? Do you bring trouble?

Randall Most certainly not! I . . . I trust my visit will be the means of avoiding anything untoward. (*He turns away from her*)

Nicola Then there is the risk of trouble. I could tell! It's in your face—in the way you stand. What is the matter?

Randall (*stiffly*) I refuse to tell you! My business can only be discussed with Colonel Hallam.

Nicola I'm not really interested. But you know how you look to me? Like a man who has been sent on an unpleasant errand.

Randall (*surprised*) But that's what I am! (*He regards her speculatively*) That's exactly what I am!

Rex comes in by the double door and pauses when he sees them

Rex Oh, I see you've met.

Nicola Yes, we've met. (*She moves up to Rex and looks back at Randall*) Mr Cooper has come in the hope of saving trouble but he doesn't seem particularly confident. Good luck, Mr Cooper.

Nicola goes out. Rex closes the door

Rex (*as he comes over to Randall*) Is anything wrong?

Randall I'm afraid there is. I have just come from a specially convened meeting of the Church Council.

Rex Should I have been present? I don't recall receiving a notice . . .

Randall No, no. The meeting was called in your absence. The Council wished to discuss their reactions to—to recent events at Stanton Manor.

Rex What events? (*He sits on the couch and indicates the armchair*) Sit down. Get your breath back and tell me why you're in such a state.

Randall Thank you—I'd rather stand.

Rex As you please. Now then . . .

Randall This, I assure you, is most painful to me. (*He turns away to avoid Rex's enquiring glance*) I am charged with delivering the deliberations of the Council. Please remember that I am only a spokesman.

Rex I'll do my best.

Randall (*moving down and still avoiding Rex's eye*) The Council weighed the available evidence and decided that you have been guilty of infamous conduct in introducing this young woman into your family circle.

Rex (*rising*) Who decided? Who called this meeting in the first place?

Randall Admiral Heathbridge was the prime mover.
Rex That old hypocrite! (*Indignantly, he strides up to the window*) Did you know that he keeps a widow half his age in Bayswater?
Randall I have heard of some such arrangement. But the circumstances are somewhat different.
Rex (*rounding on Randall*) They are indeed! I'm doing what I can to right a wrong done years ago and I'm doing it publicly. But it's in order, I suppose, for the Admiral to pop up to town and spend as long as he likes with his mistress providing he's discreet about it.
Randall You wilfully misunderstand me. The lady in question lives at Bayswater. The Admiral does not ask the wives and daughters of the congregation to meet her.
Rex But how ridiculous! Nicola is charming, intelligent and pretty. Do you think it would harm the ladies of Medham to meet her?
Randall Possibly.
Rex What?
Randall I can only say how she appeared to me in the brief time I saw her: she seemed to me self-seeking, sly and quite without any sense of morality.
Rex You hardly saw her! Why, man, she's only a girl!
Randall No. She's a woman with her eye on the main chance—one who would let nothing stand in her way.
Rex You're either prejudiced or crazy. Let's get back to this Council meeting. What was the result of their profound deliberations?
Randall (*again avoiding his eye*) They decided you were unfitted for the post of Vicar's Warden and asked for your resignation.
Rex Did they? Did they now? And what did you, as Vicar, say in my defence?
Randall There didn't seem anything to say. The facts are self-evident.
Rex I see. So you said nothing and voted with the rest?
Randall There was no need for me to vote. The Council was unanimous.
Rex It all seems to have worked out conveniently for you. You haven't had to do anything. Like Pilate, you've simply washed your hands of the offender. (*His gesture imitates the washing of hands*)
Randall That is a blasphemous observation.
Rex Not when you consider where I stand. Until today, I was proud to be Vicar's Warden. Now anybody is welcome to my office. I gladly present you with my resignation. Is that all?
Randall Not quite. In the unhappy circumstances, it was hoped that you would see your way to giving up your pew in order to save embarrassment.
Rex Surely one of the primary objects of the Christian Church is to bring the repentant sinner to God so that he may be forgiven? Isn't that your duty? Are you going to cast me out of the Church just when I stand most in need of salvation?
Randall (*uncomfortably*) It isn't a question of casting you out. I cannot keep you out of the Church but the Council felt that it would inflame public opinion if you continued to occupy such a prominent pew.
Rex The rent of my pew is, I believe, paid up to the end of the year?

Act II

Randall You mean you will not give it up?
Rex More than that. Tomorrow morning I shall occupy it with my family. With all the members of my family. Will you convey my decision to the Council?
Randall I will do so. But I think you are unwise in risking ostracism for yourself and your family.
Rex We risk nothing for neither I nor my family will acknowledge the presence of the Council. (*He sits on the couch*) We shall ostracize them.
Randall I have done my part. I thought it my duty to warn you.
Rex Oh, yes. By all means do your duty. If that is all, please go. I find you loathsome.

Randall has almost reached the double door when he seems to recollect something. He returns to Rex

Randall There is one other matter. (*He produces an envelope and offers it to Rex*) Would you give this to Harriet?
Rex (*rising and stepping back*) Oh, no! I will do nothing of the kind! I can guess what's in that letter. But you'll tell her yourself. (*He goes to the bell-push and presses it*) For once, you'll have to face up to the consequences of your actions.
Randall I merely wished to spare Harriet pain.
Rex Not you. You were, as usual, sparing yourself. I see you for what you are. You're not a priest—you're a place-seeker. You set out to find a comfortable living and, having found one, you determined to keep it—at whatever cost.

Lillah comes in

Tell Miss Harriet that Mr Cooper wishes to see her.

Lillah curtsies and goes out

Randall You're very hard on me. I don't know what entitles you to pronounce judgement on me.
Rex Just this—whatever I've done, I've walked on my own two feet and lived as a man—not crawled on my belly like a slug. I haven't spent my days being lick-spittle to a pack of hypocrites.
Randall I won't stay and listen to your abuse. (*He moves to go*)
Rex (*barring his way*) You'll stay and speak your piece. When you've said it, get out and never show your face here again. (*With a violent heave, he thrusts Randall from him.*)
Randall There's no fear of that.

Harriet enters. Sensing the strained atmosphere, she glances from one to the other

Rex Randall has something to say to you, my dear. (*He goes over to the double door*) If you should lack a subject for your sermon tomorrow, I suggest you preach on the story of the praying Pharisee.

Rex goes out

Harriet (*anxiously, as she comes over to him*) What is it? Is Father angry?

Randall I have just come from a Council meeting where it was decided to ask for your father's resignation as Vicar's Warden. It was also suggested that he should give up his pew.

Harriet Because of her? Because of Nicola?

Randall I am afraid so.

Harriet And what does he say?

Randall He has offered his resignation but he refuses to give up his pew. Indeed, he threatens to attend the service tomorrow with all of you—including the young woman. It is not for me to advise you but I think you would do well . . .

Harriet But there's something else, isn't there? Father said you wanted to see me.

Randall Yes. I find this most distressing, Harriet. Believe me, I wished to save you pain. I scarcely know where to begin.

Harriet Shall I anticipate what you're struggling to say? You'd like to break off our engagement. Is that it?

Randall I'm in a very vulnerable position. This, I realize, is a most serious matter and, if I should seem to countenance your father, I should find myself in an impossible situation.

Harriet It means nothing to you that I detest this girl, that I bitterly resent her presence in this house . . .

Randall These are considerations which would weigh very little now that your father has publicly acknowledged this—this discreditable connection.

Harriet It has happened most opportunely though, hasn't it? You are provided with an excuse for ending our engagement.

Randall Surely you must see that marriage between us is out of the question under these unhappy conditions.

Harriet None of this would matter if you loved me, Randall. (*Raising her hand to silence his protest*) You never once mentioned love to me when you proposed marriage. Admiration and respect were the nearest you came to it and I suppose you have neither admiration nor respect for a woman as unhappily circumstanced as I am. (*She sighs, and moves down to the secretaire. For a moment she is silent then she turns to him*) Very well. It is over. I release you from our engagement, Randall.

Randall Thank you, Harriet. You have behaved admirably. I wish I could say as much for myself.

Harriet Shall we say that, with your nature, you could not have behaved otherwise. (*She takes her engagement ring from her finger and offers it to him*) Here, take this.

He is forced to cross the whole length of the room. Embarrassed, he accepts the ring and puts it in his coat pocket

I shall return your letters, of course, and your presents—both of them.

Randall I would much prefer that you kept the presents.

Harriet (*decidedly*) Oh, no! I could not do that. When I looked at the one and used the other, I would inevitably be reminded of you and that I would wish to avoid.

Randall Then it remains for me to say good-bye. (*He offers his hand*) You'll shake hands, Harriet?

Harriet No. (*Imperiously, she moves away*) That would suggest that there remains some kindness between us. There is none on my part. I despise you and I would like you to remember that. You'd better go now.

Randall Very well. I shall, however, remember you with kindness and I shall be happy if I can ever be of service to you. (*He goes up to the double door and turns as if for a final word but, faced by her implacable expression, he stands faltering and discouraged*)

Harriet One thing I must tell you: Gregory would have acted very differently but then he was merely a gentleman—not a practising Christian.

With a gesture of hopelessness, Randall goes
Harriet stares after him for a moment, then collapses on the couch in an agony of weeping

(*Calling out in anguish*) Randall! Oh, Randall!

Nicola enters by the small door, goes over to the couch and stands looking down at Harriet. After a moment, she lightly touches Harriet. Harriet recoils when she looks up

Nicola Can I do anything?

Harriet No. No, thank you. (*She makes a great effort at control, wipes her eyes and stands up*) You've done it already.

Harriet is still wiping her eyes when Lillah enters by the double door and hesitates on the threshold

Harriet What is it, Lillah?
Lillah Mrs Kemp-Collet is here, Miss Harriet, to see the master.
Harriet Show her in and then go and tell the master.
Lillah Yes, Miss Harriet.

Lillah goes out

Harriet pats her face and smooths her hair, but suddenly realizes the inadequacy of her efforts

Harriet Oh, I can't face her looking like this.

Impulsively, Harriet turns and runs out by the small door.
Nicola is still staring after her in surprise when Lillah ushers in Vashti Kemp-Collet, an imposing-looking woman of Rex's age, who is dressed as if for a ceremonial visit. Lillah goes

Vashti surveys Nicola from head to foot and back again

Vashti So you're the young person.
Nicola I admit to being young but I don't like being described as a person in that tone of voice—particularly by a stranger. (*Angrily, she moves up to the window*) It sounds as if you're assessing an applicant for domestic service. (*Then her hand goes to her mouth as she suddenly realizes*) Oh, you must be the aunt!

Vashti What do you mean by "the aunt"? I am Mrs Kemp-Collet and I am aunt to my sister's children. The aunt, indeed! I am not your aunt.
Nicola For which I am profoundly grateful.
Vashti How dare you!
Nicola You ought to be grateful too. I think we'd make completely incompatible relatives.
Vashti In all my life, I have never encountered such calculated impertinence.
Nicola Then you've been very lucky so far. I've had lots worse and I'm less than half your age. But you mustn't think you have the monopoly of rudeness just because you're old.
Vashti (*beside herself*) I've a very good mind to box your ears.
Nicola (*moving closer*) You'll be sorry if you did because I should certainly retaliate.
Vashti (*uneasily maintaining her ground*) Oh, would you?
Nicola Yes—and I can guarantee to hit a good deal harder than you.

Nicola and Vashti are still glaring at each other when Rex comes in by the double door

Rex What is it? (*He pauses halfway between them and looks from one to the other*) What's the matter?
Vashti This—this young woman has just threatened me with violence.
Nicola Only because she threatened me first.
Vashti (*as if Nicola had not spoken*) And she has been insufferably rude to me.
Nicola She began it when she spoke of me as "the young person". I won't have anybody speaking to me like that. I won't!
Rex (*sharply*) That's enough! There's no point in discussing this when you're both so heated. You'd better go now, Nicola. I shall speak to you presently.

Nicola starts towards the double door with irritating slowness

Vashti And is this all you are going to say to her after she has so grossly insulted me?
Rex I said I would speak to her presently. Go along, Nicola.

Rex and Vashti watch Nicola as she walks to the door and both are surprised when she turns with an apologetic air, walks a few paces to Vashti and speaks in a conciliatory tone

Nicola Mrs Kemp-Collet . . .
Vashti Yes?
Nicola I should like you to know that I have derived great benefit from your visit.
Vashti I am relieved to hear it but I cannot believe you to be sincere.
Nicola But I am. I am grateful for the instruction you have given me. Now I know just how *not* to begin an acquaintance. Thank you so much.

With a courteous inclination of the head, Nicola goes out

Vashti glares speechlessly after her. Then she rushes up to the door

Act II

Vashti (*calling*) Come here! Come back here at once! (*Irritated by Rex's immobility, she wheels round on him*) Aren't you going to call her back?
Rex No. If I did so there would be one of those tremendous shouting-matches which you so much enjoy and which invariably give me a headache. I prefer to avoid the possibility.
Vashti (*coming down to him*) Don't you think, after what you heard, that an apology is due to me?
Rex Not until I have heard both sides. I know you can be most exasperating.
Vashti (*struggling for control*) I gather that you have seen this girl only at intervals so that you cannot know her very well. Whereas you have known me for more than thirty years and, during that time—
Rex Exactly, Vashti. I have known you for over thirty years . . .
Vashti What do you mean by that?
Rex By this time I know you fairly well. In my experience, you are overbearing, obstinate, interfering and—yes, vindictive.
Vashti (*heatedly*) If that is your opinion of me, it is remarkable you have tolerated me for so long. It is astonishing to me that you have ever sought my advice or pretended affection for me. Why, you must be a thoroughgoing hypocrite!
Rex I'm nothing of the kind. And I haven't pretended affection for you. I'm genuinely fond of you. But I've had to concentrate on your qualities of loyalty, kindness and generosity.
Vashti Oh, then I have some good qualities? (*Sitting in the armchair*) Thank you very much for drawing attention to them.
Rex We all have qualities and faults. (*Smiling, and evidently bent on reconciliation*) Nobody is perfect. I am only too conscious of my failings.
Vashti Are you? Are you indeed? That is most accommodating of you. Now, if you've quite finished with my shortcomings, perhaps we can turn to yours. They might provide us with a more rewarding study. It might interest you to know how I regard you in the light of your recent conduct. (*She regards him scornfully*) To me, you're not so much a man as a rabid, ravening monster.
Rex That is surely an exaggeration.
Vashti How else am I to regard you? By acknowledging this—this . . .
Rex Daughter of the left hand?
Vashti This by-blow of yours. You have violated my dead sister's memory. Poor Elizabeth! She must have guessed what was going on at the time. No doubt it hastened her end.
Rex Elizabeth knew nothing. I kept it from her—for her sake rather than mine. So you can't accuse me of hastening her end.
Vashti I'll try to believe it. But the effort is beyond me at the moment. Do you realize what you've done? You've outraged public decency, antagonized your friends and laid your children open to corruption. Yet you stand there looking as if I were the guilty party. What have you got to say for yourself?
Rex First of all, Frances—Nicola's mother—and I were deeply in love. It is only right that I should acknowledge our daughter.

Vashti Love! Men like you don't know what it means. Lust! Lust of the flesh is all you understand. (*She rises and contemplates the portrait*) Poor Elizabeth knew what love was. She lavished hers. She squandered it on you.

Rex I don't want to excuse myself, Vashti, but the physical side of our marriage was over before I met Frances.

Vashti The physical side! (*Disgustedly, she turns from him*) How dare you mention such a thing to me? That's all your marriage ever meant to you. Elizabeth was such a spiritual creature. She, poor soul, loved beyond the merely physical but you could scarcely be expected to appreciate her. Elizabeth was wasted on you!

Rex Believe that if it comforts you.

Vashti And I am wasting my time. I had thought to bring you to a realization of where you stand at this moment.

Rex I am sorry if my response has disappointed you.

Vashti Mockery will avail you very little. It is clear you fail to comprehend the full seriousness of what you have done. I must admit that I am not greatly concerned about you but I am considerably concerned about the effect of this scandal on my nephew and nieces. You realize, of course, that the Vicar can scarcely be expected to go through with his marriage to Harriet now.

Rex He was here a little while ago and I understand he asked her to release him.

Vashti (*triumphantly*) You see? And this is only the beginning.

Rex She's better off without him.

Vashti Is she? Is that your view or hers? There is another matter which must be mentioned now—the proposed engagement between Mildred and Vivian.

Rex (*alarmed*) Vashti, for God's sake! You're not going to be so foolish...

Vashti In the circumstances, I cannot allow the announcement. It would not be in Mildred's best interests and, as her guardian, I must withold my consent.

Rex You realize, of course, that they can marry without your consent in a year's time.

Vashti They can. And, if they do, Mildred will get none of my money.

Rex I don't suppose that would disturb either of them very much. But I can see your mind is made up. I'm sorry. I don't think you should make them suffer for what is really my affair. You're making altogether too much of this. People will, I grant you, be shocked at first. But they'll come round once they begin to know Nicola.

Vashti (*grimly*) That I doubt. I doubt it very much indeed.

Rex Oh yes, they will. You are forgetting that Victoria is no longer on the throne. Life isn't as stuffy and constricted as it was. There's a new spirit of toleration today. People will come to accept this situation in time.

Vashti You are deluding yourself. (*Reflectively*) I cannot speak for the East End of London where, I understand, a very different social order prevails. I have no authority to speak for Bayswater, St John's Wood, Chelsea and the Earl's Court end of Kensington where, I believe, a

Act II

certain degree of moral laxity obtains. But I can speak for Medham and I tell you we live here—and proudly—by the standards of Queen Victoria and shall continue to do so. The dear Queen knew the value of an inflexible morality and an unimpeachable family life. While I have breath, I shall do my utmost to preserve her ideals. (*She turns to go*) Please don't trouble to see me out. (*She halts and looks back*)

Rex, standing with his back to her, does not move

Rex . . .
Rex Yes?
Vashti Do you really believe that Elizabeth didn't know about you and that woman?
Rex I'm sure she didn't.
Vashti Then why do you think she left her money to Vivian?

Vashti goes

But she has successfully planted the seeds of doubt. Rex stands for a moment deep in thought, then, reflectively, goes to a chair and sits, nodding once or twice as if to confirm a recollection

Maggie enters

Maggie Mrs Kemp-Collet is just leaving, sir.
Rex Yes. Yes, Maggie. I know.
Maggie Could you spare me a moment, sir?
Rex Of course, Maggie. Is anything the matter?
Maggie It depends how you look at it, sir. I want to give notice.
Rex Notice? Oh, no! Maggie, you've been with us so long! What should we do without you?
Maggie You'll manage, I'm sure, sir.
Rex But why? Why do you want to give notice?
Maggie It's my sister—my sister and her husband. They've taken this public house and they'd—they'd like me to help them. My sister's not strong.
Rex I see. If you must, you must. We shall miss you—miss you very much. Give me as long as you can. Housekeepers—good housekeepers—aren't easy to come by. Look, Maggie. Can't they get somebody else? Do you really have to go?
Maggie No, sir. No, I don't. It's a small place. They don't want me. But I can stay there while I look around.
Rex Then you don't have to go?
Maggie Oh yes, sir, I do.
Rex Why?
Maggie I hoped you wouldn't ask but, since you have, I'll tell you. There's Lillah. She's above herself, sir. She won't do as she's told—and you know why that is, sir. There was Fletcher. He was a decent man and you treated him badly.
Rex No, I didn't. I gave him a year's wages when he went.

Maggie I'm surprised he took them. Then there's this young lady. She took the trouble to warn me that I'd need to be careful if she were to make her home here.
Rex That's ridiculous. I'd see to it—
Maggie No, you wouldn't, sir. Nobody can make promises where that young lady is concerned.
Rex So your mind's made up, Maggie?
Maggie It is, sir.
Rex I don't like it. I don't like it at all. You may go.
Maggie Thank you, sir. (*She starts towards the door*)
Rex Maggie . . .
Maggie Sir?
Rex I could refuse to give you a reference.
Maggie That is for you to decide, sir. Isn't it a good thing that I don't have to give you one?

Maggie goes out. Rex stands staring after her. Harriet comes in. She stops short when she sees Rex is alone

Harriet Oh, I thought Aunt Vashti was here.
Rex She was here. She went a few minutes ago.
Harriet What did she want?
Rex Can't you guess? Vashti seldom misses an opportunity of making herself unpleasant. This time she ran true to form. She expressed her disapproval at considerable length.
Harriet (*her tone and expression suggesting she already knows the answer to her question*) Was that all?
Rex No. She withdrew her consent to Mildred's engagement.
Harriet I see. That was to be expected, I suppose. (*There is a silence*) Why have you brought that girl here, Father?
Rex I've told you already. I want to provide for her, to give her a home . . .
Harriet And what about us, your legitimate children? Are we to have no consideration? Are our lives to be ruined because of her?
Rex (*scornfully*) Ruined! (*He turns away from her*)
Harriet Aunt Vashti has forbidden Mildred and Vivian's engagement. You will not be surprised when I tell you that Randall has asked me to release him.
Rex I anticipated as much. He wasn't worthy of you.
Harriet Worthy or not, he's the only man who has asked me to marry him. Now, because of her, I shall die an unhappy old maid.
Rex Nonsense! You're talking nonsense! "As good fish in the sea . . ."
Harriet (*bitterly*) Nothing matters as long as she can be with you. Remember I saw you both last night. I ask you again—why have you brought her here?
Rex (*exasperated*) How many times do I have to tell you? It's natural that I should want my daughter here, isn't it?
Harriet That might be natural. (*Her voice rising*) But the way you were kissing her was not! Isn't that the real reason you want her here? (*Shrieking when he does not reply*) Isn't it?

Rex (*rushing at her*) You evil-minded slut! I'll show you!

He raises his arm to strike her, but she stares back at him without flinching.

Harriet No, you won't. Because you know I'm right.

He continues to glare at her but slowly lowers his arm

Rex You've had something of a shock. I must try to make allowances. If you're wise, you'll forget what you said. I'll try to do the same. (*He goes to the double door*)

Harriet Father . . .

Rex pauses

Until the other day I admired you more than anybody in the world. That was because I didn't know you. She was right. We were strangers to one another. Now I've seen you for what you are and I find you detestable—hateful. I shall leave this house.

Rex Do as you please. I certainly won't beg you to stay.

Rex goes out

Harriet turns from the door, moves irresolutely to the couch, then goes to the window where she stands gazing out unhappily

After a moment Lesley comes in by the double door. She is carrying an opened envelope in one hand and a letter in the other, and wears a shocked, stunned expression

Concerned, Harriet moves over to her

Harriet What is it, Lesley? Are you ill?

Lesley The post has been. I've had a letter from Harry. Not the usual one this time.

Harriet leads her to the couch and they sit side by side. Lesley gives the letter to Harriet. She reads it quickly and looks up with a troubled expression

Harriet My poor Lesley!

Lesley Harry never wrote that letter. Never in this world. He couldn't have. He wouldn't know the meaning of half the words. Somebody wrote it for him. He just copied it out and signed his name. (*She takes the letter back and, without looking at it, restores it to its envelope*) But it serves its purpose well enough. I'm dismissed like an unsatisfactory servant—discharged without a character.

Harriet is moved, lays her cheek against her sister's and puts an arm about her

Harriet But so am I. I've nobody either now. We'll go away and set up house together—somewhere where they don't know us and they've never heard of her.

Lesley (*drawing away*) What are you saying? I don't understand . . .

Harriet Randall was here only half an hour ago. He has broken off our engagement.

Lesley Randall? Randall was here?

Harriet nods

A pity I didn't see him. He was right, you know.
Harriet Right?
Lesley Yes. He said that Harry would surprise me one day.

Lesley sits nodding her head and then, with a little cry, turns, weeping, to Harriet. Harriet tries to comfort her, as—

the CURTAIN falls

SCENE 2

The same. Sunday morning

Rex, wearing morning dress, is sitting in the armchair smoking a cigar and reading a Sunday newspaper. Vivian, also wearing morning dress, comes in. He looks troubled and agitated

Rex Are they coming?
Vivian In a moment. I gave them a call as I passed.
Rex Good. We're going to be ready in good time. (*He consults his watch*) Oh, yes. We needn't start for at least half an hour.
Vivian Do you really want me to come?
Rex Of course I do. You especially. If you weren't there, they'd think you agreed with them. (*Suddenly anxious*) You don't, do you? I took it for granted . . .
Vivian No, no. I certainly don't agree with them.
Rex I don't care what the girls think—as long as they come—but I'd like to think that you are on my side. (*He looks to Vivian for response. When it is slow in coming, he goes on irritably*) Well, are you?
Vivian Oh, yes. Most decidedly.
Rex You don't sound very decided. Quite the reverse. What is troubling you?
Vivian (*turning away*) I just don't feel that I ought to be in church this morning.
Rex But you've got to be. We've all got to be there. We'll go in just after the first bell—when they've given us up. (*He studies Vivian's turned back*) You're not afraid of them, are you?
Vivian I don't want to see Mildred, that's all.
Rex That won't make any real difference, my boy. (*He rises, goes over to Vivian and puts a hand on his shoulder*) Mildred will wait. You'll see. I know what I'm talking about. She'll stand by you.
Vivian (*sulkily*) I'm not sure that I want her to. (*And he shrugs away from Rex's hand*)
Rex (*irritably, as he moves away*) Then I fail to see what's bothering you. (*He goes to the secretaire and gets rid of his cigar in the ashtray*)

Act II

Lesley, dressed for church, comes in, buttoning her gloves

Where are the others?
Lesley I haven't seen Nicola. Harriet is ready.
Rex Then where is she?
Lesley She went back for her handkerchief.
Rex (*angrily*) Harriet will forget her handkerchief when she is summoned to her Maker. I wish they'd stir themselves. I would like to say a few words before we set out.
Lesley (*with a movement towards the door*) Shall I . . .
Rex (*checking her with a gesture*) For Heaven's sake, no! You'd probably decide to change your hat or something equally stupid.

Vivian wanders aimlessly to the couch. For a moment Lesley waits awkwardly, then her expression relaxes

Lesley They're coming. I hear them.

The voices of Nicola and Harriet are heard—Harriet's is raised angrily. As they approach, they become audible

Harriet (*off*) If I hadn't seen you with my own eyes, I would never have believed it.
Nicola (*off*) But you did see me so you've got to believe it.

The double door flies open and Nicola is propelled some distance into the room. She turns as she recovers her balance and calls out

Don't touch me! Keep your hands off me!

Furiously angry, Harriet swirls in after her but is checked when Rex speaks

Rex What are you doing, Harriet?
Harriet Ask her what she's been doing. Go on, ask her. Better still, ask me. She'd probably lie to you. I went back to my room just now and found her sitting at my desk reading my diary. (*Suddenly screaming at Nicola*) Weren't you? Weren't you reading my diary?

Nicola does not answer, but returns Harriet's glare contemptuously

Rex Is this true, Nicola?
Nicola Of course it's true. Look at her face. You surely don't imagine that Harriet would be wrong in such a matter.
Rex Why did you do it?
Nicola I saw Harriet leave her room. It seemed to be my opportunity and I slipped inside. But Harriet came back and caught me. It's as simple as that. I should have been more careful—I was guilty of an error of judgement.
Rex This is no occasion for flippancy. Why did you read Harriet's diary?
Nicola (*shrugging*) This is such a dull place. Insufferably dull. One has to take amusement where one finds it. And I must say I found Harriet's diary amusing. Most amusing.

Nicola steps back and holds up a restraining hand as Harriet makes a threatening movement

Oh, it wasn't just the references to me—though I greatly enjoyed those. Such a vitriolic pen you have, Harriet dear. But all those inspired passages about Gregory! Now those I really relished! Such a remarkable man! Such an astonishing person! So very masculine and so very tender!

Harriet Why don't you tell them? Why don't you tell them and have done?

Nicola (*shaking her head*) And spoil everything for you? Oh, I wouldn't do that. I realize that you have to live with them. (*She surveys the others comprehensively*) With these strangers. Didn't I tell you that's what you were—strangers to each other?

Rex You haven't understood us if that is how you regard us.

Nicola Haven't I? Wait until you hear. Just wait until you hear. I think I understand you better than you understand yourselves. I've been finding out about you all—your little weaknesses . . . your guilty secrets.

Rex There's nothing for you to find out. We've no secrets here.

Nicola You don't sound in the least convinced. In fact, you seem most apprehensive. It's quite understandable. You know what *you* have to hide. But you're wondering about the others. In your place, I'd do the same.

Rex Nicola! Go to your room! I'll speak to you later!

Nicola (*dancing mischievously away from him*) Oh, no! No! I'm enjoying myself too much. And I won't speak to you later—I'll speak to you now. (*Mockingly, she looks from face to face.*) Oh, look at you all! What troubled consciences you must have! Everybody frightened about what I'm going to reveal. But I'll deal fairly with you. I'll promise you something: I'll tell you my secret. Mine, I assure you, is of particular and general interest. You'll see. Now where shall I begin? (*She looks from face to face as apprehension grows, and she is actually regarding Vivian when, with a pouncing movement, she suddenly switches her attention and points at Lesley*)

Lesley (*frightened*) Oh, no!

Nicola Don't be silly. It's nothing so very dreadful. Wait until you hear about the others. (*Becoming portentous*) Behind the books in the locked cabinet in Lesley's sitting room . . . (*She pauses and smiles encouragingly into Lesley's anguished face*) Behind the copies of Jane Austen, Scott, Dickens, Trollope and Thackeray—

Lesley Nicola, I beg you . . .

Nicola —are books of a kind not usually to be found in the library of a young lady. The text is shocking in the extreme but the illustrations! I was horrified! (*She raises her hands in mock horror and travesties an expression of disapproval*) Wherever did you get such naughty books, Lesley? Certainly not from dear Harry. (*Turning to Rex*) I really think the source of this—literature should be investigated, don't you?

Rex (*ignoring her and staring directly at Lesley*) Do you have these books, Lesley?

Lesley Yes, Father, I—I'm afraid I have.

Act II   49

Rex Then where did you obtain them?
Nicola No, no. Not now. (*She rushes up to him*) Investigation can wait. We'll never get to my secret at this rate. (*She faces Harriet*) Now Harriet . . .
Harriet But you said you weren't going to . . .
Nicola Ah, yes. But that was before we decided—I decided—on this game of secrets. You wouldn't like to be left out. You'd be offended. You'd be hurt, Harriet. Especially when you hear my secret. Harriet fills the pages of her diary with descriptions of her romance with Gregory—the man she met when she was staying with her Aunt Jessie in Bristol. It was a terrific affair. They were everything—everything—to each other and some of the passages are every bit as shocking as those books in Lesley's cabinet.
Harriet Don't you dare! Don't you dare say another word!
Nicola You can't silence me, Harriet. (*She stalks over to Harriet*) Don't you wish you could? (*She turns to the others*) Harriet, it seems, was feeling somewhat depressed one day last October. Or perhaps she felt the need to tell the truth to her diary—just for once. That day she confessed in its pages that there never had been such a person as Gregory. Ah! Ah!

As Harriet moves forward threateningly, Nicola retreats rapidly waving an admonitory finger. Baffled, Harriet halts

   He was a figment of her over-heated imagination. All she wrote in her diary expresses the thwarted lust and longing of a desperate female foredoomed to be a spinster from the cradle to the grave. Isn't that so, Harriet?
Harriet Damn you! Damn you to hell!
Nicola Really! (*She walks away as if shocked, then turns*) You never thought she could use such words, did you?
Harriet I'll find a way. (*Her face is averted from Nicola*) I'll find a way to hurt you.
Rex We'll have no more of this. Stop it, Nicola! That's more than enough.
Nicola Oh no, it's not. I've only just begun. I decide when we've had enough. Or are you afraid because your turn's coming?

Rex cannot meet the challenge of her glance. He looks apprehensively at the others. Harriet is turned away from him. Vivian avoids his eye but Lesley is regarding him expectantly. Hastily, he looks elsewhere

   Maybe you're not afraid. After all you were a soldier—a colonel. You may be telling yourself that you have nothing to hide. But you'd be wrong—quite wrong. You have the most to fear. (*She suddenly turns from Rex to Vivian*) Look at Vivian! Look at him!

They all look at Vivian. He is regarding her with desperate appeal

Vivian For God's sake, Nicola! Think what you're doing. You'll ruin us all.
Nicola I don't think so. No, I don't think so. (*Addressing Rex*) Ever since you told me about this family of yours, I've been curious about them. I couldn't believe that they could be quite as dull and respectable as you

made them out to be. Of course, they're not. (*She smiles round at them*) Well, I was intrigued to learn more about you all. So I took a holiday in Amberley and I kept my ear to the ground. You remember Lettice Powell, don't you, Vivian?

It is obvious from Vivian's expression that he does

Harriet (*turning to him*) Lettice Powell. That was her name! That was the name of the girl who came to see me!

Nicola Of course she did! I knew we could rely on your memory, Harriet. That was when they were putting the screw on Vivian. Her visit did the trick. He paid up all right after she'd seen you.

Rex What's all this about? Who is this girl, Vivian? Who is she?

Nicola A very wicked girl. (*She comes over to him with a confidential air*) She'd have you believe that she and Vivian made you a grandfather while you were away fighting the Boers. But they didn't. When her young man got her in the family way, she managed to convince Vivian that he was responsible. Then she produced her young man, this Stephen Knowles, who said he was willing to marry her and Vivian gratefully gave them the wherewithal to get married. And he's still paying generous maintenance for the child. (*Turning to Vivian*) Aren't you, Vivian?

Vivian stands miserably silent

Rex Is this true?

Nicola Do you need an answer? You've only to look at him. (*She goes to Vivian and pats his arm consolingly*) I can prove that it's Stephen's child, Vivian. You needn't pay them another penny.

Rex How utterly stupid you've been! Taking up with a trollop like that when my back was turned. You should have come to me. Why didn't you?

Vivian (*sullenly*) How could I? You were away at the War when it happened.

Rex Yes, yes. But when I returned . . . You should have come to me then.

Nicola And you would have advised him out of your own wider experience, I suppose. You're well qualified to do that, of course. What about May Dunnet?

Rex May—Dunnet?

Nicola Oh, come on. The girl you kept in a house in Chelsea.

Rex I turned her out if you must know. She deceived me.

Nicola But it took you a long time to find it out. She deceived you for three years—every minute of the time that you kept her. You're not very smart either, are you? (*She shakes her head*) You hardly qualify as an adviser, I'm afraid. But that's not your secret, is it? Let's get it over. Let me put you out of your misery. By the luckiest accident, I met Fletcher.

Rex Fletcher? When was this?

Nicola (*turning quickly to him*) Ah, you're interested. Two or three weeks ago. When I knew where he came from, I made a friend of him and he made a confidante of me. So I know all the circumstances connected with his leaving here.

Rex Fletcher is a scoundrel—a confirmed liar!

Act II   51

Nicola But that wasn't what you wrote in his reference.
Rex Naturally not. I didn't want to deprive him of his livelihood.
Nicola Fletcher's misfortune was that he fell in love with Lillah without realizing that she was his master's mistress. It was a great shock to him when he came into the study that night and found you and Lillah together.
Harriet Oh, no!

The others reflect her shock and incredulity

Nicola (*calmly, sitting in the armchair*) She's been your mistress for two years now. So convenient to have a girl available on the premises—one who is dependent on you. (*Suddenly raising her voice*) It's true, isn't it?
Rex (*tormented*) Of course it isn't. You know it isn't!
Nicola (*reflectively*) I suppose I could bring Fletcher here but it would take a little time . . . (*Then, her face brightening as she rises*) I know. I'll ring for Lillah. (*She moves purposefully over to the bell-push and stands with her hand poised*) Shall I? Shall I ring for her?
Rex No, no. Leave it. (*He moves away sullenly*)
Nicola It is true then?
Rex Yes—yes. It's true. (*With a pathetic return to his blustering manner*) But I cannot understand how a daughter of mine should concern herself with bringing grief and shame to her own family.
Nicola (*delighted*) But that's it! (*She comes over to him*) That's my secret!
Rex What do you mean?
Nicola I am not your daughter.
Rex Don't be ridiculous. I know you are.
Nicola How do you know?

Rex struggles for words

Come on, how do you know?
Rex Why, your mother told me. We were living together.
Nicola (*mimicking*) "We were living together." And that's your proof? "Your mother told me." Now I'll tell you. Just before you parted, Frances went back up North, didn't she?
Rex Yes. Her mother was ill.
Nicola Her mother was dead long before she met you. What happened was that Joe Ollerenshaw beckoned her and she went to him. Joe was the man in her life. The only one.
Rex He was not. You've got it wrong. She cared for me. She loved me.
Nicola I know. Better than you. Better than anybody—except her. She told me. When she found out that she was going to have Joe's baby, she told him and he agreed to marry her. She came back to you and convinced you that you were the father of the child she was going to bear. (*She pauses, looks at him with her head on one side and laughs merrily*) If you could just see your face!
Rex I'll not believe it! I'll not believe any of this!
Nicola Cast your mind back—remember how it was. Frances had you in a cleft stick. You couldn't marry her because you were married already.

Joe, as she told you, was ready and willing. So you did what she'd expected: gave her a handy sum as a wedding present and offered to pay for my upbringing. Trusting, weren't you?

Rex You're trying to hurt me. I don't know why but you're trying to hurt me. You've made this up.

Nicola I haven't. Not a word of it. You've only to check the date of my birth and you'll see that you couldn't possibly be my father.

Rex You were born prematurely.

Nicola Not me. I was a full-term baby and that can be proved. (*She surveys them with mounting satisfaction*) I tell you that I am not your daughter. (*Turning to Vivian*) So you needn't have me on your conscience any longer.

Vivian expresses relief. Neither Rex nor Lesley see any significance in this remark. Harriet, however, glances in disgust from Nicola to Vivian

I'm Joe Ollerenshaw's child and I'm glad of it.

Rex How long have you known this?

Nicola A long time—ever since I was fourteen.

Rex Fourteen? (*He shakes his head incredulously*) She told you all this when you were fourteen?

Nicola She couldn't help herself. I started asking questions when she brought me to see you. I knew Joe as my father and I was puzzled. I wanted to know who you were.

Rex To tell a child of that age . . .

Nicola I was quite precocious and we were very close. We discussed things not usually mentioned between mother and daughter.

Harriet That I can well believe.

Rex is startled and he turns to her in surprise. Still with an air of surprise, he looks at Vivian and Lesley—he had forgotten their presence. Then he faces Nicola again

Rex But I don't understand. Even if it is true, why had you to tell me? I haven't deserved it of you.

Nicola (*advancing on him*) Who says you haven't? Just because you paid for my upbringing and education, do you think you've bought me for ever? You owed that—and more—to my mother for suffering you all that time.

Rex Suffering me? Suffering? You don't know what you're saying.

Nicola (*taunting*) She had a name for you—Mr Moneybags, that's what she used to call you. "You need some new dresses, dear," she'd say to me. "Come on, we'll get them out of Mr Moneybags."

Rex Stop it! Stop it! You speak as if you enjoyed hurting me. What have I ever done that you should treat me like this?

Nicola You've done enough. More than enough. You're the sort of man I find it easy to despise. A woman-chaser who believes he has charm. And so you have—between the covers of your pocket book. And what about the sickening way you've talked about my mother, ever since I came here?

Act II   53

Rex (*moving away from her*) But I haven't! I haven't done anything of the kind.
Nicola Yes, you have! As if you'd owned her! How do you think I've borne it knowing how she felt about you? And then you bring me to this dead-and-alive hole presided over by that (*indicating Harriet*) frozen-faced creature. And why? For no very good reason. Not when you sneak into my room in the middle of the night, mauling and kissing me and calling me Frances, your own true love.
Vivian He didn't! He didn't do that!
Nicola No? Just look at him. It wouldn't have stopped there, either, if I hadn't thrown him out of my room. (*Wheeling on Rex*) Is that why you tucked me away in the private suite?
Rex Shut your mouth, you foul-mouthed slut!
Nicola I'm not. Whatever I am, I'm better than you. What was it you said when I told you about Vivian and Lettice Powell? (*Mimicking*:) "You should have come to me." (*They face each other*) For advice, I suppose. For instruction perhaps? A fine one you are to offer advice or give instruction. Being your son what chance had Vivian to be other than what you are—a dupe. (*Her voice rising*) That's you—a dupe. Tell me—how does it feel to learn you've been tricked for twenty-one years? How does it feel, Mr Moneybags?

Rex strikes her across the face

Rex Get out! Get out before I kill you, you bitch!

Nicola stands facing him fearlessly while they glare at each other. As Rex raises his hand to strike her again, Vivian thrusts between them

Vivian Don't touch her! Leave her alone!

Nicola pushes Vivian aside and continues to face Rex

Nicola (*soothingly*) It's all right. It's quite all right, Vivian. He won't hit me again and he'll regret that blow as long as he lives.

Vivian moves away with his eyes fixed on Rex who is gazing as if hypnotized at Nicola

Do you hear me? As long as you live, you'll regret it. You paid for my education. Now you'll see that I'm able to apply what I've learned. (*She turns to Lesley*) Do you remember what I told you about Joe's evenings—that I did impersonations? You lot have given me some marvellous material. I reckon my impersonation of Harriet will bring the house down.

Nicola's smiling glance comes to rest on Rex. He has not moved but stands looking crushed as stricken

As for you . . . (*She assumes a travesty of a masculine posture and achieves a comic echo of Rex's voice*) "The truth cannot hurt us." Well, you've got the truth. Do you like it? (*She laughs*) Do you feel anything now?

Laughing again, Nicola goes out

Nobody moves for a moment, and then Rex shakes himself as if seeking to shed Nicola's influence. He looks unhappily from one to the other of his children to find each of them regarding him with the same expression of bitter accusation

Rex That girl is evil. She meant to harm us from the first. Her mother wasn't like her. Not a bit like her. And she's quite wrong—wrong when she wasn't lying. She was determined to hurt me. You could see that, couldn't you? (*He goes on with diminishing confidence in the absence of response*) She's jealous because her mother loved me.

Anxiously, desperately, Rex is watching for the first sign of awakened sympathy. There is no change of expression in any of the accusing faces confronting him

She did love me! She did, I tell you! Frances loved me!

But the implacable faces of his children contradict him and, as his entreating glance rests on Harriet, she hardens her expression and shakes her head in firm denial. Suddenly, he crumples and disintegrates before their eyes. He covers his face with his hands and bursts into loud, agonized weeping. With his face still covered, he goes, weeping, to the double door. There he fumbles for the door handle and goes out shrieking

She loved me! She loved me!

Rex exits

They do not watch him as he goes. His weeping is heard for a moment or two through the closed door. Then, silence. Before it becomes oppressive, Vivian goes to Lesley who is nearer to him than Harriet. He kisses her

Vivian I'll say good-bye, Lesley.
Lesley Where are you going?
Vivian With her. With Nicola.
Lesley Go with her? After what you've just seen and heard?
Vivian Nothing that I've seen or heard alters anything. All I want is to be with her for the rest of my life—if she'll let me.
Harriet Oh, she'll let you. No doubt of that. She'll let you just so long as you've got the money. You've got plenty so you should last quite a long time.
Lesley You speak to him, Harriet. (*She goes over to Harriet and takes her urgently by the arm*) Tell him that he'd be mad to go with her.
Harriet (*removing her hand*) What good would it do if I did? He wouldn't listen. If he listened, he wouldn't understand. Look at him. He's Father's son—born to be duped by a woman—a woman like her.
Vivian That is what I expected from you. At least, you see that I have no choice. (*He goes over to her and kisses her unresponsive cheek*) Good-bye, Harriet.
Harriet (*without looking at him*) Good-bye. I wish you joy of her.

Vivian (*surprised*) Why, thank you, Harriet.
Harriet Not that you'll find any joy with her. Quite the reverse. She'll ruin you. (*She turns away*)
Vivian And I don't care! I don't care if she does!

Angrily, Vivian turns to go, but is momentarily checked as Lesley lays a detaining hand on his arm

Lesley What about Father? Aren't you going to tell him?
Vivian You tell him—or let him guess where I've gone.

Vivian strides past her and goes out, leaving her staring after him

Lesley I feel sorry for Father. I know what she meant when she said he would regret that blow as long as he lived.

Harriet, who has not watched Vivian's departure, stares bleakly ahead

Harriet She has destroyed us.

The church bells begin to ring for matins. The sisters stand listening as the chimes ring out their cheerful summons, and—

the C<small>URTAIN</small> falls

FURNITURE AND PROPERTY LIST

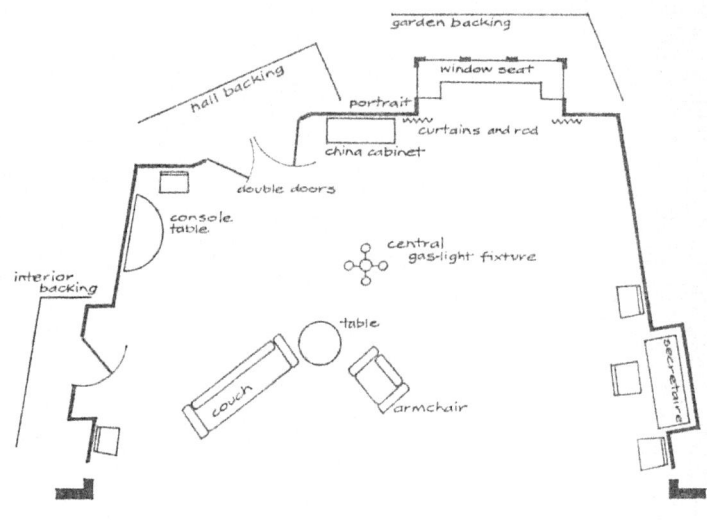

ACT I

SCENE 1

On stage:
Couch
Armchair
5 small chairs
Window seat
China cabinet. *Above it:* portrait of an attractive woman
Console table. *On it:* flower arrangement
Secretaire. *On it:* writing materials, ashtray
   Above it: bell-push
Lace curtains
Heavy window curtains
Carpet
On walls: water-colours

Off stage:
Large envelope (**Randall**)
Envelope (**Lesley**)
Tray with glass of whisky (**Lillah**)

Personal:
Harriet: chatelaine
Vivian: cigarette-holder, cigarettes, matches
Rex: key

Scene 2

Strike:
  Empty glass

Set:
  Magazine on armchair
  Bills and account books on secretaire
  Embroidery on couch

Off stage:
  Tray with whisky decanter, soda-water syphon, 2 glasses (**Lillah**)

Personal:
  Lesley: reticule with letter in envelope
  Rex: hat, coat, gloves

ACT II

Scene 1

Strike:
  Magazine, whisky tray and glass, Rex's hat, coat and gloves

Off stage:
  Envelope (**Randall**)
  Opened envelope (**Lesley**)

Scene 2

Set:
  Sunday newspaper on armchair

Personal:
  Rex: cigar, watch

LIGHTING PLOT

Interior. A drawing-room. The same scene throughout
Property fittings required: central gas-light fixture

ACT I SCENE 1: Afternoon

To open: General effect of May sunshine
No cues

ACT I SCENE 2: Evening

To open: Gas lighting on, with brightest glow around couch
No cues

ACT II SCENE 1: Morning

To open: Effect of morning sunlight
No cues

ACT II SCENE 2: Morning

To open: As Scene 1
No cues

EFFECTS PLOT

ACT I
Scene 1
No cues
Scene 2
No cues

ACT II
Scene 1
No cues

Scene 2

Cue 1: **Harriet** "She has destroyed us." (Page 55)
  Church bells ring—continue to fall of Curtain